W9-BID-550

THE ROMAN
EMPIRE AND
THE NEW
TESTAMENT

Abingdon Essential Guides

THE ROMAN EMPIRE AND THE NEW TESTAMENT

An ESSENTIAL GUIDE

Warren Carter

Abingdon Press
Nashville

THE ROMAN EMPIRE AND THE NEW TESTAMENT
AN ESSENTIAL GUIDE

Copyright © 2006 by Abingdon Press

All rights reserved.
No part of this work may be reproduced or transmitted in any form or by any means, electronic or mechanical, including photocopying and recording, or by any information storage or retrieval system, except as may be expressly permitted by the 1976 Copyright Act or in writing from the publisher. Requests for permission can be addressed to Abingdon Press, P.O. Box 801, 201 Eighth Avenue South, Nashville, TN 37202-0801, or emailed to permissions@abingdonpress.com.

This book is printed on acid-free paper.

Library of Congress Cataloging-in-Publication Data

Carter, Warren, 1955-
 The Roman Empire and the New Testament : an essential guide / Warren Carter.
  p. cm.
 Includes bibliographical references (p.   ).
 ISBN 0-687-34394-1 (binding-pbk. : alk. paper)
  1. Bible. N.T.—Criticism, interpretation, etc.   2. Bible. N.T.—History of contemporary events.   3. Church history—Primitive and early church, ca. 30–600.   4. Rome—Social life and customs.   5. Rome—Politics and government—30 B.C.–284 A.D.   6. Rome—Religion. I. Title.

 BS511.3.C38 2006
 225.9'5—dc22

2006004350

All scripture quotations unless noted otherwise are taken from the *New Revised Standard Version of the Bible,* copyright 1989, by the Division of Christian Education of the National Council of the Churches of Christ in the United States of America. Used by permission. All rights reserved.

Scripture quotations marked RSV are from the *Revised Standard Version of the Bible,* copyright 1946, 1952, 1971 by the Division of Christian Education of the National Council of the Churches of Christ in the United States of America. Used by permission. All rights reserved.

06 07 08 09 10 11 12 13 14 15—10 9 8 7 6 5 4 3 2 1

MANUFACTURED IN THE UNITED STATES OF AMERICA

To Bob Mowery
with Appreciation

Contents

Introduction

This book explores ways in which New Testament writers interact with and negotiate the Roman imperial world.

This book is not about "Roman backgrounds" to the New Testament, because it understands Rome's empire to be the foreground. It is the world in which first-century Christians lived their daily lives. It is the world that the New Testament writings negotiate throughout.

This book is not about "church-state" relations as that term has conventionally been understood. Books dealing with that topic usually discuss a few passages that refer to rulers and emperors. This book recognizes that Rome's empire does not disappear or go away when it is not explicitly mentioned. It is always there. It forms the pervasive context of New Testament writings.

This book clearly rejects the notion that Jesus and the New Testament writings are not political. When Jesus declares, "My kingdom is not from this world" (John 18:36), he does not mean, as many have claimed, that Jesus doesn't care about Rome's empire or is only interested in "spiritual" realities. His claim is about the origins of his reign or empire as being from God, not a statement about what it influences or how far it extends. The New Testament writings are clear that God's good and just purposes embrace all of life. They are also clear that negotiation with Rome's world is determined by the fact that Rome crucified Jesus. People got crucified not because they were spiritual, but because they posed a threat to the Roman system.

First-century Christians did not negotiate the empire in the context of empire-wide persecution. There was no such empire-wide, empire-initiated persecution against Christians until the third century. They did experience——for what reasons?—some local harassment and opposition. Early Christians and New Testament writers engaged the empire largely "from below" as the powerless and oppressed who had no access to channels of power, no voice, and no hope of changing the imperial system. This book looks at some of the diverse ways in which they negotiated a world in which imperial politics, economics, culture, and religion were bound up together.

Several options existed for organizing the book. I could have written chapters on each of a number of New Testament writings. I could have organized it by particular strategies. Instead, I have chosen to organize it around important imperial realities that New Testament writings negotiate. This organization highlights significant aspects of the empire that the New Testament writings negotiate. It also provides the opportunity to observe different ways of negotiation evident in various New Testament writings.

Chapter 1 describes the Roman imperial system. Chapter 2 discusses some evaluations of this system offered by New Testament writings. Chapter 3 identifies interactions with powerful imperial officials ("faces of empire"). Chapter 4 examines countryside and cities as places that express Roman power and as places in which Christians negotiate that power. Chapter 5 asks similar questions about temples. Chapter 6 considers ways in which claims about God and Jesus engage and contest Roman imperial theology. Chapter 7 looks at ways Christians negotiated basic daily matters that express imperial power, namely economics, food, and health. Chapter 8 explores three further forms of resistance to Rome's empire—imagined violence, disguised and ambiguous protest, and flattery. This discussion is illustrative and not exhaustive.

Regrettably, limits on the book's length, appropriate to the Essential Guides series, prevent printing all the New Testament passages that I discuss. It would be helpful for readers of this book to refer to those New Testament passages while reading this book.

The book can be used as a seminary or college course textbook, or by a church Bible study group or Sunday school class. It provides passages to study, insights about them, and raises questions for consideration. It provides the basis for asking hard questions about how contemporary Christians negotiate our own contexts of imperial power. The book is also a resource book for clergy and scholars interested in this emerging area of contemporary scholarship. A bibliography provides further resources for exploration as well as acknowledges some of the vast debt I owe to numerous, previous insightful studies. Limits on the book's length prevent acknowledging this debt in extensive endnotes.

Warren Carter
June 2005

CHAPTER 1

The Roman
Imperial World

The New Testament texts, written in the decades between 50 and 100 in the first century, originate in a world dominated by the Roman Empire. In places, New Testament texts refer openly to this imperial world and its representatives such as emperors (Luke 2:1), provincial governors (Mark 15:25-39), and soldiers (Acts 10). In places, as we shall see, New Testament writers speak critically about this imperial world. In places, they seem to urge cooperation with Rome. "Fear God. Honor the emperor" (1 Pet. 2:17).

But in most places they do not *seem* to us to refer to Rome's world at all. Jesus calls disciples from fishing. Jesus heals the sick. Paul talks about God's righteousness or justice and human faithfulness. None of this appears *to us* to have anything to do with Rome's empire.

Throughout this book two issues will concern us. The first involves recognizing that the New Testament texts assume and engage Rome's world in every chapter. Even when the New Testament texts seem *to us* to be silent about Rome's empire, it is, nevertheless, ever present. It has not gone away. The Roman Empire provides the ever-present political, economic, societal, and religious framework and context for the New Testament's claims, language, structures, personnel, and scenes. The New Testament texts guide first-century followers of Jesus in negotiating Rome's power that crucified Jesus.

1

And second, we will see that New Testament writers evaluate and engage Rome's empire in different ways. This variety and diversity of engagement will emerge in each chapter of this book.

At least two factors hide this Roman imperial world from us as twenty-first-century readers.

The first factor concerns the relationship between religion and politics. We often think of religion and politics as separate and distinct. Religion is personal, individual, private. Politics is societal, communal, public. Of course, just how separated religion and politics really are is debatable (think of the "political" slogan, "God bless America," or of those who seek martyrdom in the name of Islam). But in the first-century Roman world, no one pretended religion and politics were separate. Rome claimed its empire was ordained by the gods. Those whom we think of as religious leaders in Jerusalem, such as chief priests and scribes, were actually the political leaders of Judea and allies of Rome (Josephus, *Ant.* 20.251). We will continually explore this intermixing of politics and religion.

The second factor recognizes that as twenty-first-century readers, we often lack knowledge of Rome's imperial world. This lack of knowledge is very understandable because our world differs in significant ways from the imperial world in which the New Testament texts came into being two thousand years ago. Understanding Rome's world, though, matters for reading the New Testament texts because these texts assume that readers know how the Roman world was structured and what it was like. The texts don't stop to explain it to us. They don't spell it out for us.

Instead we are expected to supply the relevant knowledge. We are expected, for example, to know that when Jesus calls Galilean fishermen to follow him (Mark 1:16-20), fishing and fishermen were deeply embedded in the Roman imperial system. The emperor was considered to be sovereign over the sea and land—a sovereignty expressed in fishing contracts and taxes on the catch. Jesus' call to James, John, Andrew, and Simon Peter redefines their relationship to and involvement in Rome's world.

It is reasonable to expect first-century folk to supply the information that the texts assume, since these folk shared the same world as the authors. But it is difficult for us who read them some two millennia later and in a vastly different world. Without under-

2

standing the Roman imperial world, we will find it hard to understand the New Testament texts.

As a first step toward gaining some of this assumed knowledge, I will sketch the structure of the Roman Empire. In the next chapter, I will describe some of the ways that the New Testament texts evaluate Rome's empire. In subsequent chapters I will elaborate specific aspects of Rome's world and ways in which the New Testament writers negotiate it.

The Roman Imperial World

In the first century, Rome dominated the territory and people around the Mediterranean Sea. Its empire extended from Britain in the northwest, through (present-day) France and Spain to the west, across Europe to Turkey and Syria in the east, and along North Africa to the south. Rome ruled an estimated 60 to 65 million people of diverse ethnicities and cultures.

The empire was very hierarchical, with vast disparities of power and wealth. For the small ruling elite, life was quite comfortable. For the majority nonelite, it was at best livable and at worst very miserable. There was no middle class, little opportunity to improve one's lot, and few safety nets in adversity.

The Roman Empire was an *aristocratic* empire. This term means that a small elite of about 2 to 3 percent of the population ruled. They shaped the social experience of the empire's inhabitants, determined the "quality" of life, exercised power, controlled wealth, and enjoyed high status.

The Roman Empire was also an *agrarian* empire. Its wealth and power were based in land. The elite did not rule by democratic elections. In part they ruled by hereditary control of the empire's primary resources of land and labor. They owned its land and consumed some 65 percent of its production. They exploited cheap labor with slaves and tenant farmers. They lived at the expense of nonelites. Local, regional, and imperial elites imposed tributes, taxes, and rents, extracting wealth from nonelites by taxing the production, distribution, and consumption of goods. Taxes and rents were usually paid in goods, so a peasant farmer or fisherman literally handed over to elites an estimated 20 to 40 percent of the catch, crop, or herd. To not pay taxes was regarded as rebellion because it refused recognition of Rome's sovereignty over land, sea, labor, and production. Rome's military retaliation was inevitable and ruthless.

The Roman Empire was also a *legionary* empire. In addition to controlling resources, the elite ruled this agrarian empire by coercion. The dominant means of coercion was the much vaunted Roman army. In addition, the elite controlled various forms of communication or "media," such as the designs of coins, the building of monuments, and construction of various buildings. These means communicated elite Roman values and shaped perceptions. Networks of patronage, and alliances between Rome and elites in the provinces, also extended control, maintained the status quo, and enforced the elite's interests. It is this hierarchy and control that Jesus describes negatively, "You know that the rulers of the Gentiles lord it over them, and their great ones are tyrants over them" (Matt. 20:25).

The Emperor and the Ruling Elite

The emperor presided over the empire. He concentrated on financial and military matters (including diplomacy), both of which were crucial for preserving Roman power and for reaping the elite's enormous rewards of power and wealth. All thirteen emperors whose reigns span the first century were males. Bearing the title "Father of the Fatherland" (*pater patriae*), the emperor embodied the empire's male-dominated and male-centered structure. That does not mean that women played no role. Women in the imperial household exercised considerable influence; wealthy elite women participated in business and civic leadership; and nonelite women were involved in household and village economies. But the empire remained a male-dominated world.

Military Force

Rome's empire was a legionary empire. Emperors needed loyal legions, the army's basic organizational unit, to exercise sovereignty, enforce submission, and to intimidate those who contem-

4

plated revolt. Several emperors such as Vespasian in 69 gained power by securing support from key legions. In the first century, there were approximately 25 legions of about 6,000 troops. Legions included large numbers of provincial recruits. Along with actual battles, the use of "coercive diplomacy" (the presence of the legions throughout the empire and the threat of military action) ensured submission and cooperation. Legions also spread Roman presence by building roads and bridges, and improved productivity by increasing available land through clearing forests and draining swamps. Armies needed food, housing, and supplies of clothing and equipment for war. One source of such supplies was taxes and special levies, for example, on grain or corn from the area in which the legion was based. Elite Roman power was secured through the military at the expense of nonelites.

Elite Alliances

Emperors ruled in relationship with the elite, both in Rome and in the provinces' leading cities. Rome made alliances with client kings, like King Herod, who ruled with Rome's permission and promoted Rome's interests. The elite, with wealth from land and trade, provided the personnel that filled various civic and military positions throughout the empire, such as provincial governors, magistrates and officials, and members of local city councils. These positions maintained the empire's order and hierarchical structure that benefited the elite so much. Relationships between the emperor and the elite were complex. Since the rewards of power were great, these relationships usually combined deference to the emperor, interdependence, competition for immense wealth and power, tension, and mutual suspicion.

In Rome, power was concentrated in the Senate, which comprised some six hundred very wealthy members. It had responsibility for legislation and oversaw its members' rule exercised through various civic and military positions. The Senate included both Romans and elite provincials appointed by the emperor. Senators were the foremost elite level, but the elite also comprised two further levels based on somewhat lower amounts of nevertheless substantial wealth, the equestrians and the decurions. Members of these orders also filled civic and military positions throughout the leading cities of the empire.

Appointees carried out their offices with continual reference to the emperor in Rome. Pliny, the governor of Bithynia-Pontus on the north coast of Asia Minor in 109–111 CE, writes some 116 letters to the emperor Trajan seeking the emperor's advice on various administrative matters: securing prisoners; building bathhouses; restoring temples; setting up a fire brigade; determining memberships of local senates; making legal decisions; constructing canals, aqueducts, and theaters; granting Roman citizenship, and asking what to do about Christians who had been reported to him. Pliny's letters show his deference and orientation to doing the emperor's will. The emperor's responses make his will present in the province.

To secure appointments to such prestigious and enriching offices, members of the elite needed the emperor's favor or patronage. They competed for favor with displays of wealth, civic commitment, and influence. These displays might involve military leadership, funding a festival or entertainment, building a fountain or bathhouse or some other civic building, supplying a food handout, or sponsoring the gatherings of a trade or religious group. These acts of patronage publicly displayed an elite person's wealth and influence as well as loyalty to the emperor and active support for the hierarchical status quo. Acts of patronage also increased social prestige by creating lower-ranked clients who were dependent on elite patrons. The emperor rewarded such displays of civic good deeds (called *euergetism*) with further opportunities to exercise power and gain wealth by appointments to civic or military offices.

Emperors who did not take partnership with Roman and provincial elites seriously and were unwilling to share with them the enormous benefits of power and wealth, usually met a grisly end. Amid various power struggles, several emperors were murdered, including Caligula (37–41), Claudius (41–54), Galba (68–69), Vitellius (69), and Domitian (81–96). Others such as Nero (54–68) and Otho (69) committed suicide. Civil war in 68–69 saw four emperors (Galba, Otho, Vitellius, Vespasian), backed by various legions, claim supreme power for short periods of time. The victor Vespasian (69–79) provided some stability with two sons who succeeded him, Titus (79–81) and Domitian (81–96). The New Testament Gospels were written during these decades. Mark was probably written around 70, with Matthew, Luke, and John being written in the 80s or 90s.

Divine Sanction

In addition to ownership of resources, military force, and working relationships with the elite, emperors secured their power by claiming the favor of the gods. Their imperial theology proclaimed that Rome was chosen by the gods, notably Jupiter, to rule an "empire without end" (Virgil, *Aeneid* 1.278-79). Rome was chosen to manifest the gods' rule, presence, and favor throughout the world. Religious observances at civic occasions were an integral part of Rome's civic, economic, and political life.

Individual emperors needed to demonstrate that they were recipients of divine favor. Various accounts narrate amazing signs, dreams, and experiences that were understood to show the gods' election of particular emperors. For example, there was a struggle for succession after Nero's suicide in 68. In the ensuing civil war, three figures (Galba, Otho, Vitellius) claimed power for short periods of time before Vespasian emerged as the victor. In sustaining Vespasian's rule, Suetonius describes a dream in which Nero sees Jupiter's chariot travel to Vespasian's house (*Vespasian* 5.6). The dream presents Vespasian as Nero's divinely legitimated successor. In a similar vein, Tacitus describes the gods deserting Emperor Vitellius to join Vespasian, thereby signifying their election of Vespasian (*Histories* 1.86).

The gods' continuing sanction for emperors was both recognized and sought in what is known as the imperial cult, which was celebrated throughout the empire. The "imperial cult" refers to a vast array of temples, images, rituals, personnel, and theological claims that honored the emperor. Temples dedicated to specific emperors and images of emperors located in other temples were focal points for offering thanksgiving and prayers to the gods for the safekeeping and blessing of emperors and members of the imperial household. Incense, sacrifices, and annual vows expressed and renewed civic loyalty. The related street processions and feasting, often funded by elites, expressed honor, gratitude, and commemoration of significant events such as an emperor's birthday, accession to power, or military victories. Acts of worship were also incorporated into the gatherings of groups such as artisan or religious groups. Elites played a prominent role in these activities, sponsoring celebrations, maintaining buildings, and supplying leadership for civic and group celebrations. These diverse celebrations presented the empire presided over by the emperor as divinely ordained. They displayed and reinforced the elite's control. They invited and expressed, encouraged and ensured the nonelite's submission.

Participation in the imperial cult was not compulsory. Its celebration was neither uniform across the empire nor consistent throughout the first century. Whereas in many cities sacrifices and incense were offered *to* the emperor's image, in the Jerusalem Temple, for example, daily sacrifices and prayers were offered *for* the emperor but not *to* his image. Although participation was not required, it was actively encouraged, often by local elites who funded such activities and buildings and who served as priests or leaders of imperial celebrations. Elite men and women served as priests for the imperial cult (and for numerous other religious groups also) because they could fund the celebrations and gain societal prestige and personal power from it. Such priestly activity, eligible for both men and women, was not a lifetime vocation requiring seminary training and/or vows of celibacy. Rather, good birth, wealth, social standing, and a desire to enhance one's civic reputation were needed.

Elite Values

With the emperor, members of the elites created, maintained, and exercised power, wealth, and prestige through crucial roles: warrior, tax collector, administrator, patron, judge, priest. These roles exemplify key elite values.

• Domination and power are foremost, pervading the societal structure. These values were celebrated, for example, in the elaborate "Triumph" that took place in Rome when a victorious general entered the city, displaying booty and captives taken in battle, parading the captured enemy leader, executing him, and offering thanks to Jupiter for Rome's victory. The Triumph, such as that celebrating Rome's destruction of Jerusalem in 70 CE, paraded Rome's military might, conquering power, hierarchical social order, legionary economy, and divine blessing.

- Elites valued civic display through civic and military offices, patronage, and euergetism ("good civic actions") that enhanced their honor, wealth, and power. Their civic leadership enacted a proprietary view of the state. Contributions to society were not exercised for the maximum common good but for personal privilege and enrichment and, in turn, for the good of their heirs. These acts maintained, not transformed, political, economic, and societal inequality and privilege.

- Elites exhibited contempt for productive and manual labor. Elites did not perform manual labor but they depended on and benefited from the work of others such as peasant farmers and artisans. Slaves were an integral part of the Roman system. They were a relatively cheap and coerced source of labor whose productivity enriched the elite. Slaves provided physical strength as well as highly valued skills in education, business, and medicine. They performed all sorts of roles: hard physical labor of working the land, domestic service, meeting the sexual needs of their owners, educating elite children, and being business and financial managers of a master's estates and commercial affairs. The imposition and collection of taxes on productive activity (farming, fishing, mining, and so forth) also expressed this contempt for labor, while ensuring the elite a constant source of income without requiring their labor. This value clearly distanced the elite from the rest.

- A fourth value concerned conspicuous consumption. Elites displayed their wealth in housing, clothing, jewelry, food, and ownership of land and slaves. They also displayed it in various civic duties: funding feasts, games, and food handouts; presiding at civic religious observances; building civic facilities; erecting statues; and benefiting clients. They could afford such displays because taxes and rents provided a constant (coerced) source of wealth. The overwhelming power to extract wealth from the nonelite by taxes made the need to accumulate or invest wealth largely obsolete.

9

- A fifth value concerns a sense of superiority. This value was sustained by and expressed through the ability to subject, coerce, exploit, and extract wealth. Rome was divinely destined to rule. Others such as "Jews and Syrians were born for servitude," according to Cicero (*De provinciis consularibus* 10). According to Josephus, the future emperor Titus urges his troops to victory over Judeans by claiming that they are "inferior" and have "learned to be slaves" (Josephus, *JW* 6.37-42). Rome was superior to provincials, the wealthy and powerful elite to the nonelite, males to females.

The Nonelite

I have concentrated so far on the ruling elite, especially the hierarchical societal structure that they maintained and from which they benefited immensely. This is the world that most of the population, the nonelite, negotiated every day.

- Since the nonelite comprised about 97 percent of the population, it is not surprising that most early Christians belonged to this group.
- An enormous gap separated the nonelite from the elite's power, wealth, and status. There was no middle class and little opportunity for improving one's lot. More often it was a matter of survival. There was no "Roman dream" of pulling oneself up by one's sandal straps.
- Degrees of poverty marked the nonelite. Some made an adequate living from trade. Most scraped by either from trade, artisan skills, or farming. Most knew periods of surplus and of deprivation so that regularly many nonelites lived at or below subsistence levels. If crops failed, if taxes increased, or if the elite withheld a city's food supply and forced up prices, there was little safety net.
- Many knew regular periods of food shortages. Poor health was pervasive. Infant mortality was high, with perhaps up to 50 percent not reaching age ten. Most nonelite adults died by age thirty or forty. Elite life spans were longer.
- Urban life for nonelites was crowded, dirty, smelly, and subject to numerous dangers: floods, fires, food shortages, con-

taminated water, infectious diseases, human and animal waste, ethnic tensions, and irregular work. Rural life also knew most of these dangers. In addition, poor crop returns meant immediate food shortages, limited seed for next year, few options with which to trade for what a peasant could not produce, the likely breakup of extended families if some were forced into cities to find work, and the inability to pay taxes or repay loans, thus risking the seizure of land. Anxiety and stress about daily survival were rife. I will consider urban life further in chapter 4, and food shortages and disease in chapter 7.

Domination and Resistance

As we have seen, elites exercised *material domination* over nonelites, appropriating their agricultural production and labor. The hard manual work of nonelites and the coerced extractions of production sustained the elite's extravagant and elegant way of life. There was a further, more personal, cost to nonelites. Domination deeply influences personal *well-being and feelings*. It deprives people of dignity. It is degrading and humiliating. It exacts not only agricultural production but an enormous personal toll of anger, resentment, and learned inferiority. Moreover, elites legitimated and expressed their domination with an *ideology or set of convictions*. They asserted it was the will of the gods (see chapters 5 and 6, below). They claimed social hierarchy and exploitation were simply the way things were.

How did nonelites negotiate this world? One practical approach was to cooperate with deferential and submissive behavior. Studies have shown, though, that whenever dominating power is asserted, there is resistance. Fed by anger and resentment, this resistance can take various forms. Occasionally it comprises violent revolt such as the revolt in Judea against Rome in 66–70 CE. Usually, though, such revolts were quickly and harshly crushed.

The absence of violent revolt, however, does not mean the absence of protest. Sometimes protests took more public forms such as pilfering elite property, evading taxes, working slowly, refusing to work at all, or attacking a symbol of domination.

More often, since direct confrontations that are violent or

11

defiant provoke harsh retaliation, protests among dominated groups are hidden or "offstage." Apparently compliant behavior can be ambiguous. It can mask and conceal nonviolent acts of protest. Often protest is disguised, calculated, self-protective. It may comprise telling stories that offer an alternative or counterideology to negate the elite's dominant ideology and to assert the dignity or equality of nonelites. It may involve fantasies of violent revenge and judgment on elites. It may imagine a reversal of roles in favor of nonelites. It may employ coded talk with secret messages of freedom ("the reign of God") or "double-talk" that seems to submit to elites ("Pay to Caesar the things that are Caesar's") but contains, for those with ears to hear, a subversive message ("and to God the things that are God's"). It may reframe an elite action intended to humiliate (such as paying taxes) by attributing to it a different significance that dignifies the dominated. It may create communities that affirm practices and social interactions that differ from domination patterns. A scholar, James Scott, sums up this sort of protest with a proverb from Ethiopia: the general (or emperor or landowner or governor or master) passes by, the peasant bows, and passes gas.

Bowing seems to express appropriate deference. But apparent compliance is qualified by the offensive and dishonoring act of passing gas. This nonviolent act is hidden, though, disguised, anonymous, shielding the identity of the one who dissents. The action is not going to change the system, but it does express dissent and anger. It affirms the peasant's dignity as one who refuses to be completely subjected. It attests a much larger web of protest against and dissent from the elite's societal order and version of reality. This web of protest has been called a "hidden transcript." It offers a vision of human dignity and interaction that is an alternative to the elite's "public transcript" or official version of how society is to be run.

The New Testament writings can, in part, be thought of as "hidden transcripts." They are not public writings targeted to the elite or addressed to any person who wants to read them. They are written from and for communities of followers of Jesus crucified by the empire. The New Testament writings assist followers of Jesus in negotiating Rome's world. Because of their commitment to Jesus' teaching and actions, they frequently dissent from

Rome's way of organizing society. Often, though not always, they seek to shape alternative ways of being human and participating in human community that reflect God's purposes. Often, though not always, they offer practices and ways of living that often differ significantly from the domination and submission patterns of Rome's world. Often, though not always, they provide different ways of understanding the world, of speaking about it, of living and relating—all the while rejecting options of total escape from or total compromise with Rome's empire. This diverse and varied negotiation is the subject of this book.

CHAPTER 2

Evaluating
Rome's Empire

I n chapter 1, I described the hierarchical structure of the Roman Empire, which benefited the ruling elite at the expense of the nonelite. I also identified a number of ways in which this elite secured and enhanced its power, status, and wealth:

1. Political office. Elites controlled all political office, including civic and military positions, for their own benefit, not for the common good.

2. Land ownership. Elites controlled large areas of land. Land was basic for wealth. Elites also participated in trade by sea and land.

3. Cheap labor, whether slaves, day laborers, artisans, or peasant farmers, produced goods largely for elite consumption.

4. Taxes, tributes, and rents, usually paid in goods (and not by check or credit card), literally transferred wealth from the nonelite to the elite.

5. Military power gained territory, extended domination, and enforced compliance. Its rumored efficiency or brutality deterred revolts.

6. Patron-client relations. A complex system of elite patrons and dependent clients from the emperor down displayed wealth and power to enhance elite status, build dependency, and secure

loyalty, dependence, and submission from nonelites. Competition for power and status among elites required displays of wealth and influence in various acts of (self-benefiting) civic leadership.

7. Imperial theology. Rome claimed election by the gods to rule an "empire without end" and to manifest the gods' will and blessings. Offerings to images of imperial figures and street festivals celebrated Rome's power and sanctioned its hierarchical societal order.

8. Rhetoric. While Rome's army coerced compliance, speeches at civic occasions and various forms of writings (history, philosophy, and so forth) persuaded nonelites to be compliant and cooperative.

9. Legal system. Rome's legal system exercised bias toward the elite and against the rest. It protected elite wealth and status, and employed punishments appropriate not to the crime but to the social status of the accused.

10. Cities. Urban centers displayed Roman elite power, wealth, and status, and extended control over surrounding territory.

In this chapter we will look at how the New Testament writers evaluate this Roman imperial world. There are numerous options open to them. They could be so heavenly minded that they take no interest in it. They could be so happy to submit to it that they simply assume its existence without asking any questions about it. They could understand it as ordained by God and passively comply. They could be so opposed to it, so persuaded that it is demonic and beyond all hope that they look only to God's future. How do New Testament writers think about this world? What perspectives do they use to evaluate it?

One important source of perspectives available to New Testament writers is the Hebrew Bible. New Testament writers know traditions about God's life-giving creation of a good world. They are familiar with Israel's long history of struggles with imperial powers, whether Egyptian, Assyrian, Babylonian, Persian, or Hellenistic. They are familiar with the central events of exodus from Egypt and exile to and return from Babylon. They also know about God's commitment to justice for all, expressed, for example, through a righteous king (Ps. 72). They know traditions about Jesus' ministry in which he was crucified by Rome. These traditions often frame their evaluation of Rome's world. The writers

15

are not so "spiritually" focused or "heavenly minded" or "religious" as to claim that God is not interested in daily life in Rome's world. Rather, they evaluate Rome's world in relation to God's life-giving purposes. They place Rome's world in theological perspective and offer various theological verdicts on it.

We will look at five quite different evaluations that form a spectrum of ways of thinking about Rome's world. Subsequently, we will identify particular strategies or behaviors for daily living that these evaluations suggest.

1. The Empire Is of the Devil

The "hidden transcripts" of several New Testament texts express a strongly negative verdict on the Roman Empire as being in the control of, and as expressing the will of, the devil. Linking supernatural powers with earthly political powers was not unusual in the ancient world. Rome claimed its rule and domination was the gift and work of Jupiter and the gods. The book of Daniel understands that war on earth is paralleled by war in heaven. An angel and the archangel Michael, "the protector of your people," fights the "patron angel" of the kingdom of Persia before facing the prince or patron angel of Greece (Dan. 10:12-21; 12:1).

New Testament texts evaluate Rome's empire in the context of the struggle between God and the devil. The devil, opposed to God's good purposes, tempts Jesus to do the devil's work, not God's (Mark 1:9-11; Matt. 4:1-11; Luke 4:1-13). In the two longer "temptation" accounts in Matthew and Luke, the devil offers Jesus all the empires or kingdoms of the earth if Jesus will worship and give allegiance to the devil instead of to God.

> Again, the devil took him to a very high mountain and showed him all the kingdoms [or empires] of the world and their splendor; and he said to him, "All these I will give you, if you will fall down and worship me." (Matt. 4:8-9)

> Then the devil...showed him in an instant all the kingdoms [or empires] of the world. And the devil said to him, "To you I will give their glory and all this authority; for it has been given over to me, and I give it to anyone I please." (Luke 4:6-7)

Both accounts identify the devil as controlling the world's empires (of which Rome in the first century CE is foremost). Both present the devil as having the power to allocate the world's empires as the devil wishes. Rome, therefore, is in the devil's control. The devil is the power behind the Roman throne.

By contrast, Jesus manifests God's kingdom or empire (Mark 1:15; Matt. 4:17; Luke 4:43). Referring to God's "kingdom" or "empire" or "reign," he uses in these verses the same word that the devil uses for the world's "kingdoms" or "empires" in Matthew 4:8-9 and Luke 4:6-7. The use of the same word highlights the contrast and opposition between the two entities. Jesus asserts God's claim of sovereignty over the world under Satan's control and manifested in Rome's rule. In Jesus' exorcisms, for example, Jesus literally "throws out" the evil spirits, exhibiting God's reign to be victorious over Satan's reign (Matt. 12:28).

Mark shows Rome's empire to be of the devil in the story of the man possessed by a demon (Mark 5:1-20). The demon's name is "Legion," the central unit of Rome's military. The possessed man's life is marked by death (5:3); by a lack of control (5:3); unshackled power (5:3-4); and violent destruction (5:5), hardly a flattering picture of Rome's power. Jesus reveals the power of the demon in addressing it (5:8) and having it identify itself as "Legion" (5:9). The demon begs Jesus not to send it out of the country that they occupy (5:10). Instead, Jesus casts it into a herd of pigs that destroys itself in the sea (5:13). Significantly, the mascot of Rome's tenth Fretensis legion that destroyed Jerusalem in 70 (about the time Mark was written) was the pig. The scene shows Jesus' power over Rome and the latter's destruction.

Mark's exorcism scene presents the might of Rome as an expression of demonic power, as wrecking havoc and destruction, but as subject to God's purposes expressed in Jesus. Its removal means people can again be "clothed and in [their] right mind" (5:15). It can be noted that studies of oppressive and imperial contexts commonly show significant increases in psychosomatic illnesses and behavior attributable to demonic possession.

The book of Revelation also presents Rome's empire as expressing the devil's power and opposing God's good purposes. Revelation 12 reveals that the devil, "a great red dragon" (12:3) and "deceiver of the whole world" (12:9), actively opposes the church (12:17). In chapter 13, this dragon gives his "power and his throne and great authority" to a beast from the sea (13:12). This is the Roman Empire to whom the devil gives dominion over earth's inhabitants who worship it (13:1-10). The beast opposes God and God's people (13:6-7). Moreover, a second beast emerges who acts on behalf of the first beast. It requires worship of the first beast. It also exerts control over economic interaction among the "small and great, both rich and poor, both free and slave" by marking them on the hand or forehead (13:16). The mark signifies ownership, reminiscent of the marking of slaves (contrast the marking of God's people, 7:2-4). It indicates that all are slaves of the beasts and dragon. That is, the chapter reveals Rome's political-economic-religious system to represent the devil's rule, to be antithetical to God's purposes, and to be an enslaving system.

2. Rome's World Is under Judgment

Mark's story of casting the demon Legion out of the man not only presents Rome's empire as being under Satan's power, but also declares God's judgment on Rome's imperial order. Various New Testament texts assert that God will end Rome's rule by judging and condemning Rome's world. This declaration counters Rome's propaganda claim that it is the "eternal city" with an "empire without end."

In anticipating God's judgment, some New Testament writers employ the category of "two ages" from Jewish eschatological texts. This thinking understood this age, the present age, to be so contrary to God's purposes, so dominated by oppressive landowners, rulers, and the power of the devil, that God will judge this world and age by ending it. God will then establish a new age and world in which God's purposes are established (e.g., 1 Enoch 46–48).

Paul employs this framework. He tells the Corinthians that the "wisdom" he speaks concerns God's purposes. God's purposes are hidden from and contrary to those of "the rulers of this age." God's wisdom is "not a wisdom of this age or of the rulers of this age, who are doomed to perish" (1 Cor. 2:6). Rome's rulers and societal order are under God's judgment. Paul makes the same point in 1 Thessalonians 5. Citing the common propaganda claim that the empire had brought "peace and security," Paul reveals its falseness by speaking immediately of God's judgment on the empire. He identifies it with darkness and night and goes on to speak of God's wrath (1 Thess. 5:1-10).

John's Gospel similarly speaks in the singular of "the ruler of this age." This ruler "will be driven out" (12:31), "is coming" (14:30), and "has been condemned" (16:11). Conventionally this ruler has been understood to be the devil. But several factors suggest it also refers to the whole of the Jerusalem and Roman ruling elite allied as agents of the devil. (1) The same word, "ruler," refers to the Jerusalem leaders (3:1; 7:36, 48; 12:42); (2) the Gospel identifies these leaders as children of the devil (8:44-47); (3) the reference to the ruler who is "coming" (14:30) seems to indicate in the narrative Jesus' impending meeting with both the Jerusalem leaders and Pilate, the Roman governor (18:1–19:25); and (4) the Gospel recognizes that the Jerusalem leaders and Pilate are allies in representing and upholding Rome's order. The Jerusalem leaders claim, "We have no king but the emperor," in solidarity with the Roman governor Pilate who crucifies Jesus for threatening Rome's order (John 19:15; cf. 11:48-53). Jesus' statement in 16:11, then, that the ruler of this age has been condemned, articulates God's judgment on the devil and on the Roman order that manifests the devil's power and purposes.

The Gospels of Mark, Matthew, and Luke also use the "two age" scheme to announce judgment on Rome's world. They contain eschatological sections (Mark 13; Matt. 24-25; Luke 21), which describe signs that precede God's judgment on the present world and the future coming or return of Jesus to effect that judgment. Matthew ironically calls Jesus' coming the *parousia* (Matt. 24:3, 27, 37, 39), a term that commonly denotes the arrival of an emperor or military commander in a town. But instead of referring to an assertion of Rome's sovereignty, Matthew uses the term to assert God's rule in Jesus' coming. Matthew 24:27-31 presents this coming as a battle. Using "eagles," and not the mistaken translation "vultures," verse 28 ("Wherever the corpse is, there the eagles will gather") depicts the destroyed Roman army, represented by the symbol of the eagle that was carried into battle and was protected at all cost, as a corpse. God's judgment enacted by Jesus condemns and ends Rome's empire.

19

3. In the Meantime: Acts of Transformation

A third evaluation refuses to accept Rome's imperial order as the way that God intends the world to be structured and urges followers of Jesus to adopt practices of (limited) transformation shaped by God's purposes.

Luke presents Jesus' public ministry as one of transformation, framing it with a citation from Isaiah 61:1-2. Jesus declares he is anointed by the Spirit

> to bring good news to the poor.
> He has sent me to proclaim release to
>   the captives
> and recovery of sight to the blind,
>   to let the oppressed go free,
> to proclaim the year of the Lord's favor. (Luke 4:18-19*a*)

These verses from Isaiah with their reference to "the year of the Lord's favor" belong to the Jubilee tradition. This tradition embraced a cycle of sabbatical years (every seven years) leading to the Jubilee year (every fifty years) at the end of seven seven-year cycles. The Jubilee year envisioned the release of people from debt and slavery, and the return of land to households (Lev. 25). It was a socioeconomic mechanism that was to prevent wealth and power accumulating in the hands of Israel's elite. It was based on an understanding that the land and all the people belonged to God and were to live according to God's purposes (Lev. 25:23). It is not clear how often, if at all, it was put into practice!

By citing Isaiah 61, Luke's Jesus offers a societal vision that challenges Rome's elite-dominated, hierarchical structure. Jesus declares God's purposes, performs these transformative acts through his ministry, and commissions disciples to continue his ministry. His vision and actions, and the continuing ministry of followers, begin to repair the damage caused by Rome's world and anticipate its end with the establishment of God's purposes.

4. In the Meantime: Alternative Communities

In Rome's world, there were no opportunities to intervene in the political process, to put amendments on ballots, to form political parties, to sign petitions, or to lead mass reform movements. And the elite was certainly not going to surrender its power and wealth voluntarily. Hence New Testament texts often urge readers to form alternative communities with practices that provide life-giving alternatives to the empire's ways.

Paul, for example, urges the churches in Rome, in a city full of displays of the elite's power and privileges: "Do not be conformed to this world, but be transformed by the renewing of your minds, so that you may discern what is the will of God" (Rom. 12:2). Renewed minds involve understandings of God's verdict on Rome's world, as well as of God's purposes for a different world. Paul instructs them to form communities of mutual support, to love one another, to not be haughty with one another, and to feed rather than avenge their enemies (chap. 12). Clearly these practices differ vastly from the indebtedness and dependency of patron-client relations, from the empire's hierarchy and domination, and the execution of military retaliation. They create a very different societal experience and very different ways of being human.

Likewise, Paul affirms that the communities of believers in Rome have significantly different roles for women. In contrast to the patriarchal structure of the empire, which presented the emperor as "Father of the Fatherland" and head of a large house-hold, but consistent with evidence that some women took promi-nent civic roles, Paul recognizes significant leadership roles for women. He describes women such as Phoebe (Rom. 16:1-2), Prisca (16:3), Mary (16:6), Junia (16:7), Tryphaena and Tryphosa (16:12), Rufus's mother (16:13), and other women with language that also describes his own ministry of preaching, teaching, pastoral care, and church planting. That is, his language recognizes the legiti-mate and significant ministries of these women.

Paul also gathers a collection among his Gentile communities to alleviate the suffering of believers in Jerusalem (1 Cor. 16:1-4; 2 Cor. 8–9; Rom. 15:25-28). Four contrasts with Rome's taxing practices are immediately evident in Paul's collection: (1) the flow of resources *from* Macedonia and Achaia *to* Judea counters the flow of resources *from* the provinces *to* Rome; (2) the collection is a willing contribution rather than coerced taxation; (3) it is not given by nonelites to support extravagant lifestyles; and (4) the intent is to relieve suffering rather than cause it.

Matthew's Jesus similarly urges believers to form alternative communities with alternative practices. While "the rulers of the Gentiles lord it over" others, Jesus declares, "it will not be so among you." Instead of domination and tyranny, followers of Jesus are to live as slaves who seek the good of the other (20:24-28). John's Gospel similarly urges communal practices of mutual service (John 13:14, 34-35). James counters the culturally imitative practice of favoring the wealthy at the expense of the poor by encouraging the opposite practice. God's favor elevates the poor (James 2:1-7).

Numerous texts urge followers of Jesus to demonstrate practical mercy in alleviating the terrible misery of Rome's world. First John 3:16-17 condemns those who claim to know God's love, who have some resources ("the world's goods"), but refuse help for someone in need. Paul (Rom. 12:19-21), Matthew (6:1-4; 25:31-46), and Acts (11:27-30) urge similar acts of practical mercy. None of these practices can bring down the massive inequities of Rome's system, but they provide an alternative to elite conspicuous consumption and help its victims survive more adequately.

5. Submitting to, Praying for, and Honoring the Emperor

Other New Testament texts evaluate Rome's world in quite different ways. Perhaps most surprising is the passage in Romans 13:1-7. Only one chapter after instructing the believers not to be conformed to the imperial world, Paul urges submission to the governing authorities. We will return to this puzzling passage in chapter 8. But other writings also evaluate Rome's world more positively and urge believers to submit to it.

The so-called Pastoral Epistles, 1 and 2 Timothy and Titus, and letters such as Colossians and Ephesians, generally take an accommodationist approach to society, imitating cultural practices like patriarchal-dominated households where women are required to submit to their husbands (Col. 3-4:1; Eph. 5:21–6:9; 1 Tim. 2:8-15; Titus 2:3-10). They do not anticipate the imminent return of Jesus with any urgency, so there is little expectation of God's transformative intervention. Rather Christians are to live quiet, nondisruptive lives as loyal citizens. They are exhorted to pray for (but not to) the emperor (1 Tim. 2:1-2; Titus 3:1-2).

22

First Peter 2:17 may go further. Christians are to accept the authority of emperors and governors and are to "honor the emperor" (2:13-17). This honoring is part of a general strategy of good conduct and social cooperation that will help Christians regain a "good name." Honoring the emperor includes loyalty to the empire in every way (2:12; 3:16) except, as it is commonly interpreted, participating in prayers and sacrifices for the emperor.

But this exception may not be so clear. (1) The refusal to participate in sacrifices and prayers would seriously undermine the strategy of social cooperation that the rest of the letter urges as the way for believers to regain a good name; (2) it neglects the letter's emphasis on inner commitment to Christ in one's heart (3:15); (3) and it overlooks the fact that all Christians did not abstain from involvement with idols (1 Cor. 8–10; Acts 15:29; Rev. 2–3). The third-century Christian writer Origen recognizes that some Christians offer sacrifices as a convenient social custom but not as genuine devotion. The possibility exists, then, that 1 Peter is encouraging Christian participation in honoring the emperor (including participating in sacrifices) as a socially convenient activity while recognizing that their real commitment is to Christ. Honoring Christ in their hearts (3:15) renders the external, socially compliant actions of sacrifice harmless.

Strategies and Practices

We have noted five evaluations of Rome's world in the New Testament writings. These evaluations range across a spectrum from "of the devil" and "under God's judgment" to seeing possibilities of transformation and the formation of alternative communities. The fifth evaluation emphasizes survival and accommodation in exhorting submission to and honor for the empire. These evaluations often appear simultaneously in the same writings.

The evaluations lead to different strategies for negotiating Rome's empire on a daily basis. Understanding the Roman order to be under Satan's control, and/or subject to God's judgment, could provoke violent attacks on the empire to express God's judgment, or withdrawal from it, or indifference to it, or engaging in an indulgent lifestyle because the world does not matter. The New Testament texts do not, however, advocate violence, withdrawal, passivity, or indulgence.

Rather, their negotiation of Rome's world is more complex. Survival, engagement, and accommodation mix with protest, critique, alternative ways of being, and imagined violent judgment. Preachers like Paul move from place to place on roads constructed to move Roman troops, taxes, and trade. They preach in cities that exploit surrounding rural areas, consign people to great misery, and extend Roman control (see chapter 4). Opposition and accommodation coexist. Followers of Jesus know a hybrid existence that results from their participation in two worlds, that of Roman domination and the alternative community of followers of Jesus.

At times this mix of opposition and pragmatic survival is a deliberate strategy, a pragmatic way of "getting by" in a context where democratic processes for change are not available and without selling one's soul completely. The mix, of course, runs the risk that the various elements will not be held in tension. Cooperation brings benefits and rewards that make survival easier. Accommodation can take over. But the mix also results from other dynamics that take effect among folk subordinated to oppressive powers.

Commonly, dominated peoples do not violently confront their oppressor because they know that the latter usually wins. Rather, the dominated combine various nonviolent forms of protest with acts of accommodation. The latter often disguise acts of dissent that are self-protective, masked, and ambiguous. But such survival-protest tactics encounter another dynamic. Whereas oppressed peoples resent their oppressors and imagine their destruction, they often come to imitate them. They resent the power that is being exerted over them, yet they recognize that being able to wield power is desirable. They long for what they resist. They resemble what they oppose. Imitation coexists with protest, accommodation, and survival. We will explore these dynamics further throughout this book, but a brief example can be noted here.

As we saw in chapter 1, the Roman Empire was a legionary empire that depended on its military prowess and threat to maintain control. It is not surprising that people living in a context of military power and subordinated to its power should absorb this military ethos and language whether they want to or not. Accordingly, New Testament writings, written by people under Roman occupation, frequently employ military metaphors to describe aspects of Christian living! That is, writers borrow a pervasive way of thinking and acting in the dominating culture, a culture they often oppose, to express aspects of their alternative worldview and way of life. The way of the world, however, is so strong and pervasive that they cannot resist its influence even as they protest it and reapply the language to a different form of existence.

We noted above Paul's certainty that the empire is under judgment and that followers of Jesus should form alternative communities. Yet Paul describes himself and coworker Epaphroditus as "soldiers" in God's service (Phil. 2:25). He sees his preaching as waging war, not a "worldly war" with "worldly weapons" but with "divine power to destroy strongholds" and to take "every thought captive to obey Christ" (2 Cor. 10:3-6). The writer of 1 and 2 Timothy summons Timothy to be "a good soldier of Christ Jesus" and to be unwavering in his commitment to serve God. "No soldier on service gets entangled in civilian pursuits, since his aim is to satisfy the one who enlisted him" (2 Tim. 2:3-4 RSV). He is to "wage the good warfare" (1 Tim. 1:18 RSV).

Paul also pictures Christian existence as a battle. There are warring powers at work within Christians (Rom. 7:23). One of these powers is the flesh, which is "hostile to God; it does not submit to God's law" (Rom. 8:7). In Philippians 4:7, as part of exhorting their anxiety-free focus on God and practice of constant prayer, he assures them that the resulting peace will "garrison" or "keep the enemy (anxiety) out of" their hearts (author's trans.).

Paul applies military metaphors extensively to the life of his churches. In 1 Corinthians 9:7, in arguing that church leaders like himself should be paid, he appeals to the fact that soldiers are paid. In 1 Corinthians 14:40 he uses a military image in urging worship that is "orderly." He uses a term that denotes proper battle order. He has argued earlier in the chapter that just as an indistinct trumpet gives uncertain signals for battle, so unintelligible speech (speaking in tongues without interpretation) is not helpful for Christian living (14:8). In 1 Corinthians 15:23 he again employs a military metaphor of troops in line for battle in referring to the "order" or "ranks" of believers who constitute the "army" of the returning Christ. In military style, the return of Jesus is signaled with blowing a trumpet (1 Cor. 15:52). In 1 Corinthians 16:15 he sees the household of Stephanas as having "lined themselves up" or "ordered themselves" for service. And in Galatians 6:15 he exhorts the Galatians to "keep in step" with the Spirit (author's trans.).

A soldier's armor frequently provides imagery of Christian living. Paul tells the church in Rome to put on the "armor of light" (Rom. 13:12). In 2 Corinthians 6:7 he tells his hearers to be equipped with "the weapons of righteousness [or justice]." In Romans 1:16-17 he describes righteousness or justice as "the power of God for salvation." The image suggests believers empowered by God living according to God's purposes to restore and heal the world. The writer of Ephesians develops the armor image at length in describing a battle not against "flesh and blood, but against the principalities, against the powers" (Eph. 6:10-17 RSV). The writer selectively highlights pieces of armor. The belt (6:14) represents integrity. The breastplate of righteousness/justice signifies protection for faithfully enacting God's purposes, whereas the sandals or shoes suggest alertness and solid grounding in the faith (6:15). The shield denotes faith or confidence in God that protects against attacks with "flaming arrows" (16:16), as does the helmet of salvation and the sword or word of God (6:17-18). This defensive pose is reflected in another military metaphor in 1 Timothy 5:14, where the writer is concerned about the conduct of women believers. His reason (and surely it is a man writing!) for having younger widows marry is that domesticating them will not "give the enemy an occasion" or "base of operations" or "beachhead" from which to launch further attacks on believers.

These examples indicate the complex interaction among factors of survival, protest, accommodation, and imitation. That which exerts Roman power is imitated in texts that encourage both living with it and opposing it. But the military language is used without comment, suggesting it is deeply ingrained in these writers who live in the midst of Roman power.

Conclusion

I have noted five ways in which New Testament texts negotiate this world. Some texts view it as being of the devil and under God's judgment. Some offer visions of transformation and shape alternative communities with alternative practices. Others urge submission, prayer, and honoring behavior. Followers of Jesus employ various strategies—survival, accommodation, protest, dissent, imitation—in negotiating Rome's world.

CHAPTER 3

Ruling Faces of the Empire: Encountering Imperial Officials

In chapter 1, I described the hierarchical structure of the Roman Empire, which benefited the ruling elite at the expense of the nonelite. In chapter 2, I described five different ways in which New Testament texts evaluated Rome's world:

1. Under the devil's control;
2. Under God's judgment;
3. Needing transformation;
4. Shaping alternative communities and alternative practices;
5. To be submitted to and honored.

I sketched some of the strategies that New Testament writers employ in negotiating Rome's world.

These diverse evaluations and strategies of Rome's world need further exploration. How did followers of Jesus negotiate the various realities of Rome's empire in their daily lives? Even if one considers the empire to be under the devil's control or subject to God's judgment, one still has to live in it each day. How did followers of Jesus engage the empire's means of control on a daily basis?

Some of these questions are unanswerable, or, at best, only partially answerable. Our sources, the New Testament texts, do not address some of these issues directly. And sometimes when they do, they outline what they want Christians to do rather than telling us what Christians were actually doing. We saw this issue at the end of chapter 1 in 1 Peter's instruction to honor the emperor. Is the instruction necessary because people were not honoring the emperor appropriately, or does the instruction reinforce what they were already doing?

In this chapter, I will focus on the interactions between followers of Jesus and the first means of control identified above, the obvious faces and representatives of the imperial system (political office). In chapter 1, I emphasized that Rome's empire constitutes the world in which the New Testament writings come into being and comprise the world in which the early Christians lived their daily lives. But while the empire was pervasive, its presence was made especially visible by its rulers. How do New Testament texts portray interaction with representatives of the empire? How do these rulers relate to God's purposes? How are followers of Jesus to negotiate the empire's ruling authorities, emperors, client kings, governors, and soldiers? Again, we will notice considerable diversity in perspectives. We will begin at the top with the emperor.

Emperors

Of the ruling authorities, the emperor in Rome was supreme. The emperor journeyed to various parts of the empire, but his face was better known from coins and statues. The New Testament writers make numerous references to emperors. I will discuss seven examples.

First, as we have noticed, 1 Peter 2:13-17 urges submission to honoring the emperor and 1 Timothy 2:1-2 urges prayer for the emperor.

Second, Jesus' difficult instruction to "pay back to Caesar the things of Caesar and to God the things of God" (Mark 12:13-17; Matt. 22:17-22; Luke 20:21-26) indicates a much more ambivalent relationship. Those who question Jesus are powerful elite allies of the Jerusalem leadership allied with Rome. Angered by Jesus' attack on the temple, their power base, they want to trap Jesus so as to kill him. Paying taxes expressed submission to Rome's and the elite's sovereignty while nonpayment was regarded as rebellion. Given this power differential, hostile intent, and imperial context, Jesus answers in a way that subordinated people often do (see further, chapter 8, below). He cleverly combines loyalty and deference with his own subversive agenda. He employs ambiguous, coded, and self-protective speech to uphold payment of a coin bearing the emperor's image, while also asserting overriding loyalty to God. He balances apparent compliance with hidden resistance.

Jesus jousts with them. He does not have a coin so he asks them for one, forcing them to admit that they do not observe the prohibition against images in the Ten Commandments (Exod. 20:1-6)! Then when they have provided the coin, he irreverently asks a remarkable question about the most powerful person on the planet, "Who is this guy?!" Then he gives a very ambiguous answer: "Pay back to Caesar the things of Caesar and to God the things of God." "The things of God" embrace everything since God is creator; "the earth is the LORD's and all that is in it" (Ps. 24:1). The "unofficial transcript" says the earth does not belong to Caesar despite Rome's claims of ownership (the "official transcript") that the tax represented. Nothing belongs to Caesar. But instead of saying, "Pay Caesar nothing," he orders payment to Caesar of Caesar's things. In context, that means the coin and the tax. But the verb translated "give" or "render" literally means "give back." Jesus instructs followers to pay the tax as an act of "giving back" to Caesar. Followers "give back" to Caesar a blasphemous coin that, contrary to God's will, bears an image. Paying the tax is literally a way of removing this illicit coin from Judea. As far as Rome is concerned, the act of paying looks like compliance. But Jesus' instruction reframes the act for his followers. "Giving back" to Caesar becomes a disguised, dignity-restoring act of resistance that recognizes God's all-encompassing claim.

Third, two emperors figure in Luke 2–3. Jesus' birth occurs when the emperor Augustus, who ruled from 27 BCE–14 CE decrees a census (Luke 2:1-3). Whether such a census occurred at the time Luke claims is debatable. But the reference is crucial for framing the story of Jesus' birth. Interpreters have claimed that the reference to the census in 2:1-3 shows the empire and God cooperating to get Joseph and Mary to Bethlehem for the birth. But it is a matter of contrast and critique, not cooperation. The census is an instrument of imperial rule and domination. Empires count people so that they can tax them to sustain the elite's exploitative lifestyle. Jesus' birth in Bethlehem, "the city of David," the city

29

from which David's family originates and in which he is anointed king (1 Sam. 16; Luke 2:4, 10-11), evokes traditions about Israel's king who is to represent God's justice, especially among and on behalf of the poor and oppressed (see Ps. 72). Jesus' birth as a Davidic king at the time of Rome's census recalls God's purposes that are contrary to Rome's and threaten to transform Rome's world. In Luke 1, Mary had celebrated God's purposes in countering elite power. God brings "down the powerful from their thrones," fills "the hungry with good things," and sends "the rich away empty" (Luke 1:52-53). How God does this politically, socially, and economically transformative work is not stipulated, but the text makes no mention of violence or military intervention.

Fourth, Luke 3:1 contextualizes the ministry of John the Baptist in the reign of Tiberius Caesar, who ruled from 14 to 37 CE. In the midst of the power of Rome and its ruling provincial allies—Herod, Philip, and Lysanias (Luke 3:1-2*a*)—God intervenes to commission an agent of God's purposes. "The word of God came to John" (3:2*b*). John ministers in the wilderness and around the Jordan, places associated with God's deliverance of the people from tyranny in Egypt. John brings a message of change (repentance) and a sign of cleansing and new beginning (baptism) in anticipation of "the salvation of God" (3:6). Among those who come for baptism are agents of the empire, notably tax collectors and soldiers (3:12-14). Repentance for them does not mean ceasing their occupations and withdrawing from the empire. Rather they are to continue their occupations but conduct them with justice. They are to stop collecting excessive taxes and extorting money.

Fifth, the alliance between the emperor and provincial elites, namely the Jerusalem leaders, is demonstrated in John 18 and 19. Unlike the scenes in Mark and Matthew where Pilate manipulates the crowds, John shows him manipulating his allies, the Jerusalem leaders. Throughout the scene, there is an ongoing sparring match in which both parties score points as they negotiate each other's power. But in the end Pilate wins the contest, making them beg to remove Jesus, thereby constantly reminding them that he has the ultimate power.

Pilate has joined with his Jerusalem allies to send troops to arrest Jesus, so he clearly understands Jesus to be a threat who needs to be removed (John 18:3). But when the Jerusalem leaders bring Jesus to Pilate for execution, he pretends not to know what Jesus has done wrong. He ignores the word "criminal" and tells them to deal with him themselves (18:29-31*a*). He knows as well as anyone that this is not possible but his apparent dismissal of their concerns goads them into an important statement of dependence on him. "We are not permitted to put anyone to death" (18:31*b*).

This admission of the need for his help is music to Pilate's ears, so he taunts them further. He claims to find "no case" against Jesus (18:38). Again, he is playing games. Jesus has just made treasonous statements to Pilate that he (Jesus) has an empire, and he has not denied being a king (18:33-37). Jesus' statement that his kingdom or empire is "not from this world" (18:36) does not mean that his kingdom has nothing to do with politics or worldly matters. Rather he means that his identity and mission come from God and involve revealing God's faithful purposes or reign for life on planet earth. Pilate knows that any talk of other kingdoms or empires and kings is dangerous.

Pilate has Jesus flogged (19:1). This action renders his next statement in 19:4, that he finds no case against Jesus, hardly convincing. He is playing games. His games continue when he again tells them to deal with Jesus themselves (19:6). Their response again expresses their reliance on Pilate's help in acting against Jesus (19:7). In the meantime, Pilate asks Jesus, "Where are you from?" (19:8-12). Understanding Jesus' origin from God is a crucial recognition of his authority, revelation, and identity in John's Gospel. Jesus' nonresponse (19:9) brings a reminder from Pilate that he has the power to release or crucify Jesus. In turn, Jesus informs the noncomprehending Pilate that he has no power over Jesus except that which is given by God (19:11).

Again Pilate taunts his allies by threatening to release Jesus (19:12). But this time the Jerusalem leaders call Pilate's bluff. "If you release this man, you are no friend of the emperor. Everyone who claims to be a king sets himself against the emperor" (19:12). He cannot release one who is a kingly pretender and is therefore an enemy of the emperor. To release King Jesus would be to fail the emperor badly. Their words signal the end of the game playing. They have called Pilate to task. His job as governor is to protect the emperor's interests. They challenge him to do what he is supposed to be doing.

31

But he gets his revenge. He asks a question to which he knows the answer but he frames it with a jab ("your King") to elicit another response of dependence from them. "Shall I crucify your King?" (19:15). Their response of begging Pilate to execute Jesus exceeds Pilate's wildest dreams. They shout, "We have no king but the emperor" (19:15*b*). It is a stunning statement. With these words these elite leaders renounce their covenant loyalty to God as Israel's king and express their opposition to God's purposes revealed in Jesus. They give their total allegiance to the emperor. Pilate the governor has done a remarkable job of securing the emperor's interests with this confession of the Jerusalem elite's loyalty! And simultaneously he gets to execute a threat to Rome's order.

In this scene Pilate walks a fine line between working with his allies to remove Jesus, and taunting and subjugating them. He respects their custom not to enter his headquarters at Passover, but he elicits from them statements of their dependence on him and of their loyalty to the emperor. The scene shows John's audience that the empire is not committed to God's purposes. It cannot recognize God's agent and does not receive his revelation of God's purposes. Allegiance to the emperor competes with allegiance to Jesus. The empire is dangerous.

Sixth, the New Testament texts, as do numerous Jewish texts, commonly refer to God as "Father." John's Gospel does so some 120 times. This title often denoted the god Zeus or Jupiter, so its use for the God of Israel and of Jesus differentiates God from the patron god of the Roman Empire. Moreover, since the rule of Augustus (died 14 CE), "father" identified the emperor as Jupiter's agent and the embodiment of Jupiter's rule. He was called *pater patriae,* "Father of the Fatherland" or "Father of the Country" (e.g., *Acts of Augustus* 35; Suetonius, *Vespasian* 12). This title not only combined religion and politics, but it also depicted the empire as a large household over which the emperor, like a household's father, exercised authority and protection in return for obedience and submissive devotion.

Paul contests and redirects such claims of sovereignty and demands for loyalty. "Yet for us there is one God, the Father, from whom are all things and for whom we exist" (1 Cor. 8:6). Matthew's Gospel takes a similar approach. The Lord's Prayer begins by addressing God as "Our Father in heaven" (Matt. 6:9).

The "our" signifies the community's different allegiance. The subsequent petitions for God's rule to be established and will to be done on earth and heaven ascribe total sovereignty not to Jupiter and the Roman emperor but to the God of Jesus. Later, Matthew's Jesus undermines allegiance to the emperor as "Father of the Fatherland" by instructing, "Call no one your father on earth, for you have one Father—the one in heaven" (Matt. 23:9).

Seventh, Acts has often been understood to offer a positive view of the emperor. Arrested, Paul denies any wrongdoing against the law, temple, or the emperor (Acts 25:8). Governors Felix and Festus do not release him. So Paul exercises his right as a Roman citizen to have his case heard before the emperor (25:10-12, 21; 26:32; 27:24; 28:19). The emperor is presented as the representative of justice, the faithful defender of what is right and wrong. Paul appears as the model citizen, awaiting vindication from the just emperor, placing his faith in the empire and the emperor as its representative. The scenes seem to uphold the imperial judicial system.

But these appearances of justice and the apparent rewards of submission to the imperial system are profoundly undercut. When Acts was written in the 80s or 90s, readers knew an important piece of information. Paul was dead, probably beheaded in Rome by the emperor Nero! His appeal to and trust in the emperor had been misplaced. His submission to the emperor had shown the emperor not to be trustworthy. His appeal resulted in death. The empire did not faithfully represent justice as its propaganda claimed. It was not to be trusted. It opposed God's purposes and endangered God's agents.

Kings

The New Testament texts, including Jesus' parables and sayings, recognize that kings, along with the rest of the elite, exercised great power (Luke 22:25), waged war (Luke 14:31), enjoyed high status (Matt. 11:8), and possessed considerable wealth (Matt. 18:23-35). The parable of the unforgiving servant in Matthew 18 employs the scenario of a king who collects tribute of ten thousand talents (the amount Rome levied from Judea in the 60s BCE). He retains various clients and slaves skilled in financial matters to collect and administer the tribute, and he punishes those who do not extend to others the favors received from him (Matt. 18:23-35). In the parable of the wedding banquet, the king invites members of the elite to celebrate his son's wedding but they insult him by not attending (Matt. 22:1-14). The king punishes them, attacking and burning their city. This is a likely reference to Rome's destruction of Jerusalem in 70 CE in which the city was attacked after a siege and burned. In an act of patronage, the king then invites the nonelite to the feast. Disturbingly, God the king (Matt. 5:35) is said to imitate these kings in dealing with disloyal humans (Matt. 18:35; 22:11-14).

Along with imitation, there is also contrast and opposition. As we have noted, Rome ruled through alliances with provincial elites. One form of these alliances involved client kings whom Rome established to rule certain territory in return for loyalty to Rome. New Testament texts refer to several client kings from the Herodian dynasty who ruled Judea and Galilee. As those who enforced and benefited from the unjust and oppressive societal order, these kings often appear in the New Testament texts as murderously resistant to God's purposes manifested in Jesus and through his followers like the disciples and Paul. Followers are warned of the lengths to which kings (including emperors) will go to protect their privileges against challengers (2 Cor. 11:32; Matt. 10:18; Luke 21:12).

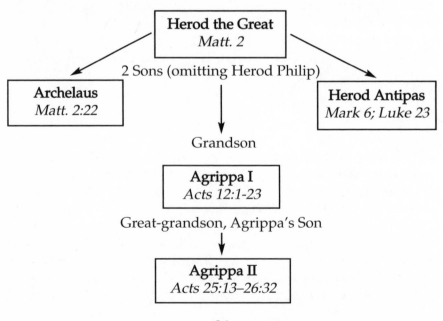

Herod "the Great" (37–4 BCE) appears in Matthew 2. He is the king who opposes God's purposes by trying to kill the newborn Jesus who has been commissioned to manifest God's saving purposes (1:21-23). The magi's announcement of a newborn "king of the Jews" threatens Herod since he is Rome's appointed "king of the Jews" (2:1-3; Josephus, *Ant.* 16.11). Matthew 2 reveals Herod's various attempts to defend his power, cataloging his elite strategies of allies, spies, lies, and murder that maintain oppressive structures:

- He uses alliances to gain information from the local Jerusalem leaders (2:4-6);
- He exerts his power to recruit the magi as spies or secret agents, sending them to gain intelligence about Jesus' birthplace (2:7-8*a*);
- He engages in spin, deceiving the magi by lying about his motives (2:8*b*);
- He employs violence after learning that the magi deceived him. He orders soldiers to kill the innocent and defenseless male infants in the region of Bethlehem so as to remove any threat (2:16).

In addition to these actions, echoes of various versions of the Exodus story of Pharaoh's opposition to Moses emphasize Herod's sustained opposition to God's purposes.

- Herod—like Pharaoh—kills infants to protect his enslaving power.
- Jesus—like Moses—escapes his murderous efforts.
- Jesus—like Moses—has a mission to deliver the people.
- God thwarts Pharaoh's and Herod's plans to kill God's agent of salvation. Instead Matthew 2 highlights Herod's death, referring to it three times (2:19, 20, 22).

Matthew 2:22 mentions Herod's son Archelaus briefly but negatively. After his father Herod's death, Archelaus rules Judea "in place of his father Herod." That is, Archelaus continues Herod's harsh rule and opposition to God's purposes being worked out in Jesus. Because of this continuation, Joseph, faithful to his task to protect Jesus as God's anointed agent, fears to go to Judea and settles in Galilee (2:22-23).

Herod's other son, Herod Antipas, continues the family's opposition to God's purposes in Galilee (Mark 6:14-28; Matt. 14:1-12; Luke 9:7-9). He has John the Baptist, God's prophet who prepares people for Jesus, arrested and beheaded after John criticizes Herod Antipas for marrying his brother Philip's wife Herodias contrary to the Torah (Lev. 18:16; 20:21). Antipas reappears nears the end of Luke's Gospel where he questions and ridicules Jesus (Luke 23:6-12).

The opposition to God's purposes continues in Herod's grandson and nephew of Herod Antipas, Agrippa I, the Roman-appointed king of Judea (41–44 CE). He attacks the Jerusalem church, killing James and arresting Peter to please the elite (Acts 12:1-5). But God delivers Peter from prison (12:6-19) and punishes Agrippa. The people of Tyre and Sidon petition Agrippa for favor and food, flattering him as a god. Herod receives the acclamation. God strikes him down, has worms eat him, and kills him (12:18-23). That is, God punishes this misplaced receiving of worship. The implications for an empire in which emperor worship was spreading are clear.

Agrippa I's son, Agrippa II, appears near the end of Acts as a much less resistant figure. Friends with Festus, the Roman governor of Judea (Acts 25:13, 23), Agrippa II displays his power and status by being accompanied by the elite, "the military tribunes and prominent men of the city" (Acts 25:23). Agrippa II listens sympathetically to Paul's preaching. He declares Paul to deserve neither imprisonment nor death (Acts 25:13–26:32).

Evident in the scenes involving (most of) the Herods is their opposition to God's purposes, defense of the status quo, and violence against God's agents. These characteristics belong to a larger biblical tradition of negative presentations of and suspicion about kings as opponents of God's purposes and agents (cf. Deut. 17:14-17; 1 Sam. 8:9-18). This tradition is employed in Acts 4:26. The Jerusalem church prays after Peter and John have been arrested and released. Their prayer interprets the events in relation to this larger negative tradition about rulers. In words that echo Psalm 2, they pray, "The kings of the earth took their stand, and the rulers have gathered together against the Lord and against his Messiah." They go on to reference the action of Herod and Pilate against Jesus. The phrase "the kings of the earth" commonly denotes rulers and nations opposed to God's purposes and people, as well as God's sovereignty over them (Pss. 76:11-12; 102:12-17; cf. Matt. 17:25).

In contrast to these kings, Jesus is presented as a king who represents God's just and triumphant purposes. Jesus is agent of God's reign or kingdom or empire (Matt. 4:17). Matthew 21:5 quotes Zechariah 9:9, part of the vision of Zechariah 9–14 in which God establishes God's reign over the resistant nations. This role inevitably involves conflict with Rome's empire. We have seen the impact on Herod of the magi's question about the newborn "king of the Jews" (Matt. 2). The passion narratives emphasize Jesus' crucifixion as "king of the Jews" (Matt. 27:11, 29, 37, 42 ; John 19:3, 14, 15, 19, 21). Since only Rome established client kings as allies to uphold the elite-dominated status quo, "everyone who claims to be a king sets himself against the emperor" (John 19:12). Jesus is crucified as a royal pretender, one who claims for himself an illegitimate title and threatens Rome's order. He is punished, as were others who claimed the title of king.

The proclamation of Jesus' significance as the agent of God's rule also causes problems for early church leaders. After Paul and Silas preached in Thessalonica, Jason and other believers were dragged before the city authorities and charged with "acting contrary to the decrees of the emperor, saying that there is another king named Jesus" (Acts 17:7).

The book of Revelation combines a number of these elements about kings in its disclosures about the nature of Rome's empire and of God's purposes (cf. 10:11):

- It introduces Jesus as "the ruler of the kings of the earth," asserting God's sovereignty over the power of the Roman emperor and its client kings (1:5).
- The "kings of the earth" (under Rome's influence, 17:18) along with "the magnates and the generals and the rich and the powerful"—the elite of the empire—are subject to God's wrath and condemnation (6:15-17). Their economic, commercial, and political dealings are condemned as unjust and demonic (17:1-6; 18:1-3, 9-13).
- Kings are agents of demonic spirits by resisting God's just purposes (16:12-14; 18:1-3).

37

- Kings battle against God and are defeated (16:12-16; 19:17-19).
- God's rightful and just sovereignty over the kings and the earth prevails (15:3; 19:16).
- Kings pay homage to God (21:24).

Governors

Provincial governors comprised another face of imperial power. The senate or emperor appointed governors from the elite. In alliances with local elites, governors represented Rome's authority and interests. They exercised enormous power in keeping order (i.e., submission to Rome), collecting taxes, building public works, commanding troops, administering justice, imposing the death sentence on those who threatened Roman elite interests, and keeping local elites satisfied. No doubt some governors tried hard to fulfill their roles well, but the sources often attest governors to be self-serving and self-enriching in exercising harsh and exploitative rule.

New Testament texts focus on encounters with governors in two arenas—between Jesus and Pilate, and between Paul and several governors in Acts. Each of the Gospels narrates the exchange between Pilate and Jesus in different ways. We looked at John's account earlier in this chapter as Pilate and the Jerusalem elite struggle with one another and express loyalty to the emperor. Here we will look at Matthew's account, where the emphasis falls on Pilate and the crowds (Matt. 27:11-26).

Pilate was governor of Judea from 26 to 37 CE. Often interpreters claim that the Gospels depict Pilate as weak and indecisive, intent on letting Jesus go but forced into executing him by the Jerusalem leaders. One interpreter goes so far as to claim that Pilate is politically neutral in Matthew's scene, which is devoid of any political pressures on him! But these claims make little sense given the strategic role, crucial responsibilities, and enormous power of governors. Pilate exercises life-and-death power. Having the power to put someone to death is not a neutral act. It is a very politically charged act. Pilate rules in alliance with the Jerusalem leaders. His task is to defend Rome's interests. He administers "justice" that protects Rome's elite interests against provincial troublemakers. He exercises this power, as we have seen from

John's account, with his Jerusalem allies even when the relationship is strained and contentious. These realities must shape our
reading of Pilate's interaction with Jesus.

When Pilate's Jerusalem allies bring him Jesus, charged with
being "king of the Jews," for execution, Jesus' fate is sealed (Matt.
27:11-14). The narrative signals this in 27:3*a*. When the Jerusalem
leaders hand Jesus over to Pilate, Judas "saw that Jesus was condemned." There has been no "trial," no meeting between Pilate
and Jesus yet, but Judas knows that the elite work together to
defend their interests. Two factors ensure Pilate will execute Jesus.
One factor concerns keeping his allies happy by respecting their
wishes. The second factor concerns the content of the charge. To
claim to be "king of the Jews" without Rome's assent is to pose a
political threat and to be guilty of treason.

But to execute a kingly pretender is risky. Pilate knows that
Jesus' crucifixion might provoke a violent uprising. Pilate needs to
know how much support there is for Jesus.

In verses 15 through 23 Pilate conducts a poll to assess the
strength of support for Jesus. He knows that since his allies are
jealous of or threatened by Jesus, Jesus must endanger the elite
way of life (27:18). He offers a public bait and switch with
Barabbas. His allies manipulate the crowd to shout for Barabbas's
release as the price of Jesus' execution (27:20-21). Pilate tests their
support by asking several times about Jesus. The crowd calls for
his execution (27:22-23). This is a masterful piece of work by
Pilate. Aided by his Jerusalem allies, Pilate polls the crowd and
manipulates them into demanding what he already intended to
do, thereby disguising his will as theirs (27:24-26).

But the narrative is equally skillful in exposing Pilate's work.
(1) Mrs. Pilate testifies that she has learned in a dream that Jesus is
"righteous" or "just" (27:19). The word in Matthew's Gospel
attests faithfulness to God's purposes. She ironically announces
that Jesus' faithful challenge to Rome's way of structuring the
world accounts for his death. (2) Pilate washes his hands of Jesus,
blaming the people and having them take responsibility (27:24-
25). But the narrative's references to Pilate's questioning of Jesus
as "king of the Jews," to the Jerusalem elite's manipulation of the
crowd, and to Pilate's polling of the crowd reveal the self-serving
nature of Pilate's and Rome's rule. It protects elite power and

privileges against a provincial threat. The narrative reveals that Roman justice is all washed up.

Not surprisingly, Matthew's Gospel warns followers about the power of governors (and kings), but promises them aid from the Holy Spirit in defending themselves (10:16-18; cf. Luke 12:11-12).

In discussing John's account of Pilate and Jesus, I noted above that in the tussle between Pilate and his Jerusalem allies, both parties elicit statements and actions of loyalty to the emperor from each other (19:12, 15). In a subsequent scene Pilate continues to taunt and subordinate these allies. He insists on putting a sign on Jesus' cross in three languages saying, "Jesus of Nazareth, the King of the Jews" (19:19). Such identification is intended to intimidate and compel compliance by reminding people of the futility of rebellion. The Jerusalem leaders want to modify the notice. They want to distance themselves from Jesus and from any notion of rebellion. So they propose it be edited to read, "This man said, 'I am king of the Jews.'" But Pilate refuses. He will not allow any such distancing. But ironically neither he nor his allies understand the truth of the proclamation that the notice makes. This scene underlines the message of the previous scene involving Pilate, Jesus, and the Jerusalem allies. The empire is not committed to God's purposes. It cannot recognize God's agent and does not receive his revelation of God's purposes. The empire is dangerous.

Paul's encounters in Acts with four provincial governors are more mixed. The first involves Sergio Paulus, appointed governor of Cyprus by the senate (Acts 13:4-12). The governor becomes a believer when he witnesses Paul perform a miracle by blinding a court magician. The second concerns Gallio, governor of Achaia in Greece (Acts 18:12-17). Synagogue leaders, likely members of the local elite, accuse Paul before the governor of teaching contrary to the law. Gallio refuses to intervene in this intra-Jewish matter and dismisses them. Others then beat the synagogue leader Sosthenes in front of the governor, but he does nothing to protect the leader. His sanctioning of anti-Jewish violence is hardly a reassuring picture of a fair-minded governor ever vigilant for peace and justice for all.

The third and fourth encounters involve governors of Judea, Felix (52–60 CE) and Festus (Acts 24–25). Exhibiting considerable interaction between these governors and their allies, the Jerusalem leaders, the scenes demonstrate rule that is more interested in pleasing elite allies than securing justice. Felix hears elite accusations against Paul, keeps him in custody, hears him preach, but does not release him (chap. 24), partly so as to not alienate the Jerusalem elite. Verse 24 indicates that Felix hopes to receive a bribe from Paul for his release, but in its absence Paul remains in prison.

Governor Festus (60–62) replaces Felix. Festus shows himself biased toward the Jerusalem leaders, his elite allies, so Paul appeals for his case to be heard in Rome (25:9-12). Festus agrees even though he and Agrippa II cannot find any guilt (25:25; 26:30-32). Neither risks alienating the Jerusalem leaders by intervening to free Paul.

The governors in Acts do not actively pursue believers. When they encounter Paul, their responses range from welcoming him (Sergio), to disinterest (Gallio), to inaction (Felix and Festus). Whereas Gallio is quite dismissive of synagogue leaders, Felix and Festus seem more interested in not offending their Jerusalem elite allies than in enacting justice. We will consider the roles of urban elites further in chapter 4.

Soldiers

Whereas most folk had little direct encounter with emperors and governors (though of course they lived daily with the consequences of their rule), soldiers probably provided the most visible face of Rome's power for local residents. For example, three to four legions, or about fifteen to twenty thousand troops, were stationed in the important Christian center, the city of Antioch in Syria, with an estimated population of about one hundred and fifty thousand. References to military action (Matt. 22:7; Luke 21:10, 20), groups of soldiers (John 18:3; Phil. 1:13), the Praetorium guard in Rome (Acts 28:16, 30; Phil. 1:13; Ephesus), and soldiers with various duties (cavalrymen, Acts 23:32; Rev. 9:16; spearmen, Acts 23:23) and of diverse ranks pervade the New Testament texts depicting them as enforcers of Rome's order.

We noted in chapter 2 that the name of the demon in Mark 5:1-20 is "Legion" (5:9, 15; Luke 8:30). This is the name of the key unit in the Roman army comprising some six thousand soldiers. Interestingly, the heavenly angels are divided into legions. When

Jesus is arrested, he forbids his followers to use any violence. He indicates that he could ask God to send "twelve legions of angels" (72,000!) but he will not ask (Matt. 26:53). Other military units include a *speira,* comprising up to six hundred soldiers (Cornelius, Acts 10:1), a guard unit (at the tomb, Matt. 27:65), a small detachment (Herod and soldiers mock Jesus, Luke 23:11), and a squad of four soldiers (four such squads guard Peter, Acts 12:4).

Military personnel of various ranks appear. Tribunes were often of elite status. In Mark 6:21 they are among the guests at Herod's birthday party. They usually numbered six per legion and commanded one thousand men. One commands a *speira* that arrests Jesus and takes him to the chief priests (John 18:3, 12). Tribunes are especially prominent in Acts 21 through 24 (see 21:31-33, 37; 22:24-29; 23:10, 15-22; 24:22). They maintain order, arrest and guard Paul, and cooperate with the Jerusalem elite and the Roman governor. Acts 23:23 identifies the chain of command, "Then [the tribune] summoned two of the centurions and said, 'Get ready to leave...with two hundred soldiers.'"

Centurions numbered about sixty per legion, commanding eighty to one hundred men. They had considerable military experience and often some social status. They appear in four contexts. (1) A centurion in Capernaum, recognizing Jesus' authority, seeks Jesus' healing power. Luke's account notes his alliance with and patronage of the local Capernaum elite (Matt. 8:5-13; Luke 7:1-10). (2) At the cross, a centurion discerns Jesus' identity as "Son of God" (Matt. 27:54; Mark 15:39) and "righteous" (Luke 23:47). The centurion attributes to Jesus terms usually associated with the emperor. (3) Acts 10 and 11 narrates the conversion of Cornelius, "centurion of the Italian Cohort" (ten cohorts per legion) as a demonstration of God's graciousness to Jew and to Gentile (Acts 11:12, 17-18); (4) Centurions are prominent in the arrest (Acts 21:32), attempted whipping (22:22-29), custody (23:16-24), and escort of Paul to Rome (Acts 27). Public order, military power, local alliances, and Roman justice are clearly interconnected.

Soldiers of ordinary rank also enact Rome's power. "Soldiers of the governor" mock, torture, and crucify Jesus (Matt. 27:27; Mark 15:16-20; Luke 23:36; John 19:2, 23, 25, 32, 34). But in raising Jesus, God mocks Rome's military power, turning the soldiers appointed to keep Jesus dead as "dead men." They cannot guard against

God's life-giving power no matter what their bribed testimony (Matt. 28:1-15). Similarly, soldiers act against Christian leaders. God's power thwarts the soldiers who guard the arrested and imprisoned Peter (Acts 12:3-19). Herod Agrippa attempts to restore order by killing them. Soldiers, including cavalry and spearmen (Acts 23:23), arrest, escort, and guard the imprisoned Paul from Jerusalem to Caesarea to Rome (Acts 21–28). Some soldiers seek guidance from John the Baptist about their conduct in the army. By not urging soldiers to abandon their weapons, John the Baptist accepts troops as inevitable. John instructs soldiers to use their power moderately without "threats or false accusation" (Luke 3:14).

Rome's military power is pervasive, but followers of Jesus are forbidden to use violence against it. Matthew's Jesus instructs disciples to disrupt the use of military power as a weapon of imperial control by combining extravagant compliance with nonviolent protests that undermine military authority (Matt. 5:41; see chapter 8's discussion of some forms of protest). Jesus rebukes a disciple who uses violence to counter Jesus' arrest. Jesus could ask God for "twelve legions of angels" to fight his arrest but this is not God's way (Matt. 26:53). John's Jesus reminds Pilate that his followers could fight his arrest with violence but will not do so because Jesus' kingdom represents God's purposes among humans ("not from this world," John 18:36).

But Christians engage in their own warfare. Given the pervasiveness of the Roman military, it is not surprising that New Testament texts use military images to depict Christian living, as I noted at the close of the last chapter.

CHAPTER 4

Spaces of Empire:
Urban and Rural Areas

R ome controlled a vast amount of territory—from England in the north, across Europe to Judea and Syria in the east, and through Spain and across northern Africa to the south. About 60 to 70 million people lived within this territory, with perhaps 5 to 7 percent living in cities. Jesus' ministry engaged small towns and villages in Galilee such as Nazareth, Cain, and Capernaum. The Gospels do not mention the significant urban centers of Sepphoris and Tiberias. Jesus travels to the areas surrounding the cities of Tyre and Sidon in Syria (Mark 7:24-30) and south to Jerusalem (Mark 10–11). As the movement spreads, followers appear in cities such as Antioch, Ephesus, Smyrna, Pergamum, Thyatira, Sardis, Philadelphia, Laodicea, Philippi, Thessalonica, Corinth, and Rome.

What role did cities play in Rome's empire, and how did Christians negotiate urban imperial life?

These questions have a further complication. Urban life had significant impact on and interaction with the surrounding countryside and their networks of small villages. Christian writings such as Philippians, Ephesians, or Revelation, associated with the urban areas named above, also addressed Christians living in surrounding rural areas and villages. Other writings such as 1 Peter were addressed to Christians in the widespread areas of five provinces that included both urban and rural inhabitants. Some scholars have suggested that Mark's Gospel originated in Galilee and addressed its largely rural village life (see 6:6, 35, 56).

This arrangement of a city surrounded by dependent villages is reflected in the description of Jesus' visits to "the villages of [the city of] Caesarea Philippi," (Mark 8:27; cf. Luke 24:13) and to the area surrounding the cities of Tyre and Sidon (Mark 7:24-31; Matt. 15:21-22). King Herod kills the baby boys in Bethlehem and its surrounding area (Matt. 2:16). Jerusalem's control extends throughout Judea and Galilee. The temple-based ruling elite in Jerusalem send representatives to Bethany, between Jerusalem and Galilee, to investigate John the Baptist (John 1:19-28). Pharisees and scribes from the same elite group travel to Galilee (perhaps Gennesaret or the surrounding area, Matt. 14:34) to question Jesus (Matt. 15:1).

Our questions, then, need to be expanded: What role did cities and the countryside play in Rome's empire, and how did Christians negotiate urban-rural life in Rome's empire?

Gospels

One System: Urban and Rural Areas

What was the relationship between urban and rural areas in Rome's world? In part each area depended on the other. The Roman Empire was an agrarian economy with land as the primary resource. Rural areas provided the food and other products required by cities. Cities consumed rural production, offered necessary skills, engaged in trade and commerce, and provided centers for imperial administration and security.

This view, though, is too simple. It ignores the hierarchical and exploitative structures and dynamics of the empire outlined in chapter 1 above. The empire's urban and rural areas were deeply embedded in these sociopolitical structures. Their economic and social life reflected the inequalities discussed in chapter 1. Cities were centers of elite power and extended their political, societal, economic, and religious control over surrounding areas and villages.

Throughout the empire, the small governing group of about 2 to 3 percent of the population, often urban based, controlled most of the land and its production. They owned large estates worked by slaves. They collected rent, usually paid in kind, from peasants. They increased their holdings by foreclosing on defaulted loans. They traded surplus for needed resources and profit. They redistributed peasant production to cities, to their own larger estates and households, and to temples. One estimate suggests that 2 to 3 percent of the population consumed some 65 percent of production. Their economic control reflected their political power and exerted enormous influence on how most of the population lived.

The Gospels frequently depict the centrality of land and agriculture under elite control. Jesus refers to practices of sowing (Matt. 13:3-9), to crop sabotage by an opponent who plants weeds (Matt. 13:24-30), and to harvest time (Mark 4:26-29). People squabble over inheritances (Luke 12:13-14) and indebtedness (Luke 12:58-59). An elite person increases his landholdings, presumably outside the city and through agents or slaves and perhaps through default and foreclosure (Luke 14:18). Another has purchased five yoke of oxen, enough animal power for perhaps one hundred acres. If this is half of his arable land, his (minimally approximate) two hundred acres is very much larger than small peasant holdings of up to about six acres (Luke 14:19). Absentee landowners employ administratively skillful slaves to manage and increase their master's wealth (Matt. 24:45-51; Luke 12:36-48; 19:11-27). Some elite landowners keep their land and wealth in the family through inheritances (Luke 15:11-32). Some build bigger barns for their crops (Luke 12:16-21). They own hardworking slaves from whom even more is expected (Luke 17:7-10). They hire day laborers from a city or village marketplace to work in a vineyard (Matt. 20:1-16), or they rely on the labor of their sons (Matt. 21:28-32). Through their agents, they take violent and fatal action against tenants who themselves use violence to refuse handing over their rent payment in the form of a percentage of the yield (Matt. 21:33-46).

The small ruling group exercised their self-benefiting control through a group (called *retainers*) who serviced elite interests. Soldiers kept order; priests ensured divine blessing on productivity; craftsmen provided various services; merchants traded production and procured necessary supplies; and village elders oversaw the tasks and negotiated with other villages and authorities. The remaining 90 percent or so of the population did the actual physical working of the land.

Clearly the losers in this vertical, hierarchical, and exploitative system were peasant farmers, urban artisans, and unskilled workers. Most peasants lived in small villages where households worked small areas of land that they owned or rented. Elites used rents and taxes to siphon off their production. Peasant labor, much despised by elites, sustained extravagant elite lifestyles. The elite's demands disrupted village patterns that cultivated communal emphases. Especially vulnerable was the practice of reciprocity whereby village households sustained one another through the fair and equal exchange of goods (see Luke 11:5-10). Likewise, village pressures that hindered anyone from getting ahead by accumulating more than others were countered by the necessity of looking out for the interests of one's own household.

Vulnerability to forces outside their control, severe poverty, and powerlessness pervaded village existence. Peasants struggled to produce enough from small landholdings to feed extended households and animals, barter for other required goods, ensure seed for the next planting, pay taxes and/or rents, and repay loans. Sometimes elites offered acts of patronage to alleviate the struggle—foregoing a rent payment, lightening a tax demand, or financing a village festival or feast. However, such actions of apparent kindness and goodwill disguised the exploitative redistributive system. They placed villages in further debts of gratitude and dependence.

The ruling group managed this urban-rural economic system to display, protect, and improve their own power, wealth, and status. Housing, clothing, transportation, food, education, manners, nonmanual work, and so forth were status markers. These markers emphasized the gap between "those with" and the vast majority of "those without."

Cities were organized geographically to underline elite control and social hierarchy. Political, commercial, religious, social, and residential aspects of urban life were closely connected. Urban centers featured buildings of political-religious power such as administrative buildings, a forum, and temples. Other buildings such as theaters, stadia, temples, and markets (*agora*) provided gathering places and opportunities for elite control through

47

entertainments, rhetoric, religious observances, and trade. Elite housing tended to be surrounded by those who provided them with necessary services and who carried out their will.

Those with no power or skills, having only their labor to sell, occupied the geographical margins of cities in cramped and unhygienic conditions. Often these people included peasants dispossessed of land through foreclosure or forced into the city because the small family landholding could no longer sustain the household. Multistoried buildings provided a vertical form of these power arrangements with the poorest and unskilled in top floors.

This urban geography and these sociopolitical arrangements are evident, for example, in the parable of the great banquet (Luke 14:15-24). Having been rejected by three elite invitees, the host orders his slave into "the streets [or squares] and lanes of the town" to invite "the poor, the crippled, the blind, and the lame" (verse 21). When the city's nonelite poor does not fill his banquet hall, he sends the slave out again. The slave goes to those who are even more socially and geographically marginal—those outside the city walls on the highways and under the hedges. These are not peasants in rural villages but the dispossessed and beggars seeking to eke out a living. Their existence is so far removed from the host's elite urban world and they have been so damaged by it that they need to be coerced into entering it. We will further consider the impact of this elite system on the nonelite in chapter 7, below.

Elite and nonelite interactions were limited, but were dominated by patron-client relationships. These relationships extended elite control through favor and dependence. They rewarded the compliance of craftsmen and laborers with the necessities of daily survival, namely opportunities for further work and small favors. Elites also extended patronage to civic groups. They practiced "euergetism" or "civic good works" such as sponsoring the regular meals and gatherings of guilds of artisans and workers (called *collegia*), burial associations, or other voluntary associations. They financed city entertainments, provided food handouts, and paid for buildings or fountains or statues in a city. These activities had great payoff. They increased the elite person's visibility, honor, and power. They obligated or indebted nonelites with dependence and gratefulness. They reinforced the hierarchical structure of submission and dependency.

The activities and control of the ruling group spanned both cities and countryside. Both arenas offered the empire's elite households numerous opportunities to maintain and enhance their sociopolitical status and power. Holding political offices within the elite-controlled city governance provided one significant outlet, as did patronage and displays of their wealth and power. Conspicuous consumption of resources, exhibited in an extravagant lifestyle, required the continual transfer of wealth to the elite. Elite households gained the cash necessary for this extravagant way of life from rents on land, loans to peasants and to artisans, investments in intercity trade and commerce, and inheritances, as well as rent from houses, apartments, shops, and warehouses. They exploited both urban centers and surrounding rural areas. They created "mini-economies" that interacted with other households and embraced urban-rural and urban-urban sociopolitical and economic interactions.

The Gospels and Acts evidence the power and social control of urban-based elites. Herod invites to his birthday party "the great ones," military leaders, and "the first ones" or "leading men" of Galilee (Mark 6:21). Luke associates these "leading men" with chief priests and scribes in the Jerusalem temple (19:47). In Acts, the high-status women and the "leading men" of Antioch of Pisidia act against Paul and Barnabas to maintain civic order by expelling them from the city (Acts 13:48-51). In Acts 25:2, the chief priests and "the leading men" from Jerusalem visit the Roman governor Festus and speak against Paul. In verse 23, the leading men accompany King Herod Agrippa and his sister Bernice to the governor Festus in Caesarea to hear Paul.

Other elite figures uphold Roman interests and societal order against those who threaten those interests and order. In Philippi, the local rulers and magistrates beat and imprison Paul and Silas for "advocating customs that are not lawful for us Romans to adopt or observe" (Acts 16:19-24). They later apologize when they learn that Paul and Silas are Roman citizens (16:35-40). In Thessalonica, further social disorder breaks out and Paul and Silas are accused of "acting contrary to the decrees of the emperor, saying that there is another king named Jesus" (Acts 17:1-9). One man, Jason, is taken before the civic authorities (called *politarchs*). Further riots break out in Ephesus involving the temple of

49

Artemis, but the town clerk calms the riot and urges action through legal channels (19:23-41; see chapter 5, below, for discussion). In these situations, urban elites maintain civic order and protect their interests against any civic, economic, or political threat to their power.

Critique and an Alternative

It is in this elite-controlled, hierarchical urban-rural world of empire that first-century followers of Jesus lived. At times, the Gospels use these realities to instruct followers about God's ways. Just as slaves, for example, must be ready for an absent master to appear at any time, so followers must be ready for Jesus' return (Matt. 24:45-51). Just as an angry master punishes a slave who has experienced a tax break but who denies mercy to another, so God will punish one who has experienced God's forgiveness but who does not forgive another (Matt. 18:23-35). The Gospels also offer guidance for how Christians might negotiate this urban-rural imperial world.

One Gospel strategy involves understanding Rome's world for what it is, namely exploitative and enriching for the elite, destructive for the rest. Jesus names the realities of self-benefiting elite rule that further depletes the poor when he says, "To those who have, more will be given; and from those who do not have, even what they seem to have will be taken away" (Luke 8:18). Slavery and poverty are givens. In a parable, a slave rightly (and boldly) comments to a very wealthy landowner, "You take what you did not deposit, and reap what you did not sow" (Luke 19:21; cf. John 4:37; 1 Cor. 3:9). In the accounts noted above involving elite figures who protect civic order, followers are warned to be careful. Elites use their power to protect their own interests by killing God's agents, punishing them, or sending them out of cities. Sometimes by doing nothing, they expose them to further hardship.

In Mark 11:12-14, 20-24 (Matt. 21:18-22), Jesus finds a nonproductive fig tree, curses it, and it withers. The story is located between Jesus' entry to Jerusalem and his judgment on the temple. This context suggests that the fig tree symbolizes the Jerusalem urban elite with control over the temple and over much agricultural activity throughout Judea and Galilee (see discussion in chapter 5, below). Fig trees with fruit conventionally signal God's blessing (Num. 20:5; Deut. 8:7-8). This fig tree, with leaves but no fruit, signifies the absence of God's life-giving blessing from this elite-controlled system that causes so much misery for most of the population. A withered fig tree depicts God's judgment on their system (Jer. 8:13; 29:17).

In Matthew's Gospel, this judgment is depicted in the parable of the king and the wedding banquet for his son (22:1-14). Matthew's version differs in some significant ways from Luke's parable of a man (not a king) who hosts a great dinner (not a wedding, Luke 14:15-24). The most significant response centers on the king's response when people refuse his invitations. Like the man in Luke's story, the king becomes angry (cf. Matt. 22:7 and Luke 14:21). But unlike Luke's man, Matthew's king sends troops, kills the people, burns their city, and then invites people from the street to come to the wedding (22:7). This action seems out of proportion to the offense, and destroys the sequence between verses 6 and 8. Fire often denotes judgment (Matt. 13:30, 40), and burning cities was a common way of punishing a defeated enemy. Rome burned Jerusalem after its defeat in 70 CE (Josephus, *JW* 6:249-408). Matthew writes into the parable judgment on the city's leaders for rejecting God's son, Jesus.

Jesus criticizes the wealthy elite who store up their abundance for their own use while most of the population lacks food. The "rich man" who plans to build larger barns for his grain and goods is a fool because in ignoring God's just and life-giving purposes for all creation, he is not "rich toward God" (Luke 12:16-21). Jesus challenges a very rich ruler to sell what he owns and redistribute his money to the poor (Luke 18:18-27). Jesus warns people against the scribes (Luke 20:45-47). Scribes were members of the elite, with power based in education and training in the law. Their role was to interpret the traditions and apply them to everyday life, hence they had great influence. As allies with other elite groups such as chief priests (20:19), they used their power to enrich themselves at the expense of others. Jesus cites their ability to "devour widows' houses" for which "they will receive the greater condemnation" (20:47).

These specific criticisms of elite exploitative power fall within a larger pattern that emphasizes God's judgment on Rome's world and reversal of it at Jesus' return, and establishment of God's purposes. As I noted in chapter 2, the Gospels regard Rome's empire as devilish (Matt. 4:8; Luke 4:5-8) and declare it will be replaced in God's judgment by God's reign or empire (Matt. 24:27-31; Mark 13:24-27; Luke 19:11-27).

That coming eschatological judgment includes very physical, material, and economic transformation. Abraham speaks to the rich man condemned in judgment: "During your lifetime you received your good things, and [the poor] Lazarus in like manner evil things; but now he is comforted here, and you are in agony" (Luke 16:25). Land will be restored to those who currently lack adequate resources. In the beatitude of Matthew 5:5, Jesus cites Psalm 37 to assure the powerless poor, the meek, that God will end the oppressive ways of the rich and powerful. Because of God's intervention, they will inherit the land or the earth. Similarly in Mark 10:29-30 Jesus promises, "There is no one who has left house or brothers or sisters or mother or father or children or fields [lands], for my sake and for the sake of the good news, who will not receive a hundredfold now in this age—houses, brothers and sisters, mothers and children, and fields, with persecutions—and in the age to come eternal life." The age to come in which God's purposes are enacted involves socioeconomic reorganization and reward for followers of Jesus.

But interestingly, it is not only a matter of waiting for this eschatological judgment. In the passage from Mark, Jesus points to the hundredfold increase in household and land as already taking place in the present. A major strategy for engaging Rome's world in the present is the creation of households and social experience that offer an alternative to elite imperial practices. Instead of an emphasis on blood relations, Jesus focuses on "fictive" kinship among his followers and upholds the kinship values of peasant households. Labor ("brothers, sisters...") and resources ("houses...land") are not hoarded for one's own advantage but exist for the benefit of others. Jesus elaborates the same approach in Luke 6:30-36 in urging followers to meet the needs of others by sharing possessions and lending, even if repayment is not possible, thereby renouncing obligations of reciprocity so valued in elite interactions. Acts of mercy, prayer for God's transforming work, fasting, and continual focus on enacting God's empire and its justice will mean that "all these things"—what one eats, drinks, wears—will be provided by God both now and in the new age (Matt. 6:25-33). Instead of domination, service for the good of others is the way of life (20:24-28). Communal support and mutual service provide coping strategies until the final judgment.

Paul's Communities

The communities of believers founded by Paul must also negotiate their rural-urban contexts. Paul's letters to them offer some insight and guidance.

Thessalonica

Since 146 BCE, Thessalonica, a city of perhaps forty to fifty thousand, had been the capital of the Roman province of Macedonia. The Roman governor resided there along with his support staff and garrison of soldiers. Some wealthy Romans were among the city's elite. Elected (elite) magistrates (called *politarchs*), a council, and a popular assembly governed the city. Ethnically the city probably comprised mostly Macedonians. Acts 17:1-9 suggests an active Jewish community, but there is no evidence of Jewish presence until the third century. Various gods such as Zeus and Apollo were worshiped along with mystery cults (Kabirus) and healing gods (Asclepius). A temple to the emperor Augustus was part of the active celebration of the imperial cult.

First Thessalonians, written in the late 40s, gives some clues to the various ways Paul's converts negotiated their urban environment. Paul refers to supporting himself there by working (1 Thess. 2:9), and exhorts them to work with their hands "as we directed you" (4:11). The emphasis on work suggests the basis of his ministry was an artisan workshop (perhaps owned by Jason mentioned in Acts 17:1-9). In the workshop, more than on street corners or in the marketplace, he gave instruction to "each one" (2:11). The letter does not mention slaves. The exhortation to self-sufficiency in 4:12 would make little sense if slaves or freedmen, still obligated to their masters, were part of the believing community. The absence of references to wealthy patrons or to strife among socioeconomic or ethnic groups within the church suggests a small group of mainly artisan converts (15 to 30?), perhaps meeting in an artisan workshop.

The letter frequently mentions opposition to Paul's preaching (2:2) and the believers' suffering or persecution (1:6; 2:14; 3:3-4, 7). There was no empire-wide persecution of believers in the first century, so their suffering or distress originates in local conflicts. The reference to their "turning to God from idols" (1:9) probably accounts for the conflicts. Other people—family members, fellow workers, friends—probably saw their "turning" as dangerous because it risked reprisal on the city, on households, on business, and on personal survival from spurned and wrathful cosmic powers.

Moreover, to renounce city gods and not participate in celebrations of the imperial cult were seen as acts of disloyalty and subversion. Paul's reference to their commitment to God's kingdom or empire would have sounded suspicious in suggesting that they follow another king or emperor (2:12). In 4:15 he refers to Jesus' return as a "parousia," a word that commonly designated the arrival of the emperor or imperial official or general in a city. The image subversively presents Jesus as the rightful ruler returning to claim sovereignty. In 5:3, by speaking of Jesus' coming as destroying Rome's world (see chapter 6, below), Paul mocks a common claim of Roman rule that it had established "peace and security."

These subversive claims and the action of renouncing idols probably caused significant tensions and strained relationships between the group of Christ believers and others in the city. Perhaps things deteriorated when several believers died before Jesus' return (4:13-18), leading to doubts among the believers and mocking from outsiders that the believers' claims of salvation from death made no sense. Insults, broken relationships, economic isolation from people refusing to do business with them, verbal abuse, and perhaps threats of physical violence seem to comprise the conflict. Twice Paul suggests that Satan, invisibly at work behind the scenes, is responsible for the conflict (2:18; 3:5).

The conflict may have involved more than spats within their neighborhoods. There are signs that it was civic and public, at least for some. For instance, in 2:14-16, Paul says they suffer from their "compatriots." He goes on to compare this suffering with actions of the Jerusalem elite in rejecting God's messengers, Jesus, prophets, and Paul. The "compatriots" in Thessalonica, then, would be the city's ruling elite who are opposing the believers. How and why would the elite get involved in conflicts with a small group of artisan believers?

In 5:15 Paul tells the believers not to repay evil for evil. The inclusion of this instruction suggests that some had done so. Whereas some seem to have become despondent in their faith (3:1-10; 5:14), other believers may have retaliated or escalated the conflict (5:15). How would they do so? In 5:14 Paul writes, "admonish the disorderly/disruptive" (author's translation). The usual translation for the last word is "the idle," but laziness does not seem to be an issue. Rather, the word commonly means the "disorderly" or "insubordinate," and can refer to civic disturbances. Perhaps some had reported the believers to the city magistrates after the believers had abandoned idol observance and the imperial cult. Maybe the magistrates took action against some believers, pressuring them to participate in cultic activity, perhaps by fining them. Or perhaps some, either believers or opponents, had tried to raise this situation in the city's popular assembly. Or perhaps this group of artisan believers had gone on strike to protest their treatment, causing civic disorder. (There is evidence from other cities of bakers and linen workers striking, causing disorder.) Interestingly, in 4:11-12 Paul advises them to live "quietly… and to work with your hands." The first phrase has the sense of withdrawing from political action and life, thereby diminishing conflict; the second might indicate Paul's exhortation to them to continue to work.

Paul's general advice to the believers is to keep their heads down and not draw attention to themselves, thereby behaving "properly" toward outsiders (4:11-12). This approach will reduce the conflict. But he also reassures them that they are caught up in God's purposes (1:4; 2:12) and that their final salvation is sure (4:13-18; 5:9-10, 23-24). This commitment makes them different from their surrounding society concerned with idols (1:9-10) and lustful passions (4:4-5), and lacking hope (4:13). He constantly underlines their identity as a distinct family or household of "brothers and sisters." He refers to them by this term some seventeen times in the eighty-eight-verse letter (1:4; 2:1, 9, 14, 17, and so forth; 5:12, 14, 25-27). And he urges them to sustain one another's faithfulness in encouraging, upbuilding relationships (3:12; 4:18; 5:11, 13-14). He assures them of God's continued working among them (3:11-13). Continually he places their present circumstances in the context of God's endgame. Jesus' return means judgment on those who rule and who cause the believers trouble, and the establishment of God's purposes (1:10; 5:1-10).

Corinth

Corinth was the capital city of the Roman province of Achaia. The city had been destroyed in 146 BCE and had been resettled and rebuilt as a Roman colony in 44 BCE. By the 50s of the first century CE, the population was perhaps between 80,000 and 130,000, including some 20,000 in the area surrounding the city. The city was ethnically and religiously diverse. Its sociopolitical structure was typically hierarchical with a small number of elite families controlling the city's power and wealth. How did believers negotiate this Roman city?

Paul had founded the church around the year 50 and stayed in the city about eighteen months (Acts 18:1-17). The community of Christ believers was ethnically mixed with Jews (1 Cor. 7:18; 9:20-21) and Gentiles. The latter, with both Greek and Roman names, had converted from Greek and Roman religions (1 Cor. 8:7-10; 12:2). Though the Acts account indicates considerable conflict with the Jewish community, 1 Corinthians does not attest either external conflict with a synagogue or internal conflict between Gentile and Jewish believers.

Although ethnic conflict seems to be absent, there are, nevertheless, significant conflicts and divisions within the church with groups committed to different leaders (1:10-11). These conflicts involve in part some issues of doctrine or spirituality, but mostly they seem to center on lifestyle issues resulting from decisions about how to negotiate their society. Some advocate significant accommodation, whereas others prefer a more separatist, even ascetic lifestyle. Paul opposes the former.

The church comprised both elites and nonelites. In 1:26, Paul describes them by saying, "Not many of you were wise [or educated] by human standards, not many were powerful, not many were of noble birth." He means, of course, that some did belong to Corinth's elite group. We know the names of at least two of these elite figures. Erastus held political office as city treasurer and spent his own money in an act of civic beneficence by paving an area east of the theater (Rom. 16:23). Gaius "hosts" the whole Corinthian church, suggesting that he was a leading patron for meetings either in his large house or in premises he hired. He is presented as an equal of Erastus and patron of Paul (1 Cor. 1:14; Rom. 16:23). There are other elites who are no longer identifiable, some of whom could well be women.

Many of the issues Paul addresses concern to a significant degree elite behaviors and social practices. It seems that there are power struggles and debates over lifestyle among the elite believers as they maintain their elite societal status while they also work out the implications of their Christian commitments. Often we think of these Corinthian believers as being deliberately difficult for Paul. But it is more helpful to remember that they are in a new situation. They do not have centuries of Christian tradition to guide them about how to conduct their daily lives in an appropriate Christian manner. They learn as they go along.

In the opening four chapters, Paul defends his way of speaking and preaching the gospel (2:1-5). Rhetoric was a major elite concern. It was not only a sign of education but it also provided a skill necessary for demonstrating one's prestige and for securing one's societal influence. Paul's refusal to employ a high rhetorical style has offended and embarrassed some who do not find him a worthy teacher but prefer Apollos. The nature of this dispute suggests that some elite members see the church as another place to extend their influence and gain honor for themselves in patron-client relations.

In chapter 5, Paul criticizes a man for sexual immorality. His lack of criticism for the woman suggests she is an outsider. The fact that the church has done nothing about the man suggests he is a powerful elite member. In chapter 6, Paul complains that members are settling disputes in court. What the disputes are is not clear. In all likelihood they involve elites who are either in dispute with one another—perhaps over property or business contracts—or in dispute with nonelites (default on loans, nonpayment of rents, and so forth).

In chapters 8 through 10 Paul discusses participation in cultic meals in temples. These meals may involve honoring the imperial cult, celebrating the important Isthmian games centered in Corinth, or seeking the favor of another god or goddess. Such activity was crucial for elites to maintain their societal status. So, too, were private dining occasions where elite status, power, and wealth were demonstrated and reinforced (10:27-30).

In 11:17-34, the Lord's Supper highlights the social divisions in the church. Some elite members celebrated the Lord's Supper in terms of their cultural practices of patronizing the meals and gatherings of artisan guilds and other collegia or associations. Meals commonly reinforced social hierarchy with differing qualities of food, tableware, and service for guests of different status. At the Lord's Supper elite members reflected social divisions and reinforced their status with abundance while others—the nonelite—did not have enough (11:18-22, 33-34).

These practices attest to the presence of elite members among the Corinthian believers (1:26). They also suggest significant cultural accommodation and imitation. These believers import their cultural practices into the church and behave in conventional social ways. They continue their quest for honor, status, and power regardless of the gospel and the impact of their behavior on nonelites in the church. Unlike Thessalonica, the church has little conflict with its imperial cultural context because it copies it, not challenges it.

Paul sees these behaviors as inconsistent with the gospel. The central issue, from Paul's perspective, seems to be not the problem of the church in the world, but too much world in the church. Paul challenges their behaviors and values. He urges more distance from their cultural practices and the formation of distinctive Christian practices about which they can be united (1:10-11).

Fundamentally, he uses the narrative of Jesus crucified, risen, and returning, to help them understand the gospel and to relativize the claims of Corinthian culture. References to Jesus' crucifixion (1:17-28) and resurrection and return (chap. 15) frame the letter. Jesus' crucifixion shows the fundamental opposition of the Roman system, with its emphasis on noble birth, power, wealth, status, and public office, to God's purposes. The "rulers of this age," both human and cosmic, were responsible for Jesus' death. They do not understand Jesus' death as the revelation of God's power and wisdom, and as the turning point of the ages (1:18–

2:13). The current age with all its displays of elite power is passing away under judgment (7:29-31; 10:11). Jesus' resurrection means the new age is underway. The Corinthians' behavior is to be guided by the spirit until Jesus returns to establish God's empire and purposes over all opponents (15:20-28).

Accordingly, Paul exhorts distance from cultural practices, though without total withdrawal from society (5:9-13). The distinctive practices that he wants will certainly disrupt and disadvantage elite members socially if they follow his teaching. In chapters 5 and 6, for instance, he demands action against the immoral man, regardless of his social status. In the church, elite members are accountable for their actions, not immune because of their status. The gospel requires moral and ethical standards that override cultural accommodations. He scorns their use of the courts by reminding them of their future role in the eschatological judgment (6:1-5). They should have their own judicial processes.

In chapters 8 through 10 he forbids their involvement in cultic festivals and meals in temples. Such syncreticism is not compatible with distinctive Christian affirmations (1 Cor. 8:6). Nonattendance at civic festivals presents a major challenge for elite members. But Paul does allow attendance at dinner parties with nonbelievers (10:27-30).

He strongly rebukes their ways of celebrating the Lord's Supper shaped by cultural practices, and urges vastly different, much more egalitarian practices that honor the nonelite (chap. 11). Their worship is to reflect not cultural hierarchies but the Spirit's presence whereby all are graced and empowered to contribute to worship as expressions of love for one another (chaps. 12–14). The collection for the poor in Jerusalem introduces distinctive patterns of economic behavior (16:1-4). Paul invites them to be in solidarity with the poor not for their own advantages of patronage but to provide relief. In contrast to the empire's vertical and dominating structures centered on Rome, he urges relief that reverses the flow of taxes and tributes to Rome and that recognizes the solidarity of the Corinthians—including the elite—with other subject people.

Throughout, in addition to reminding them of God's yet-to-be-completed purposes, he seeks to set in place an alternative communal identity and way of being in their world. He reminds them that they are a "holy" or "sanctified" people (1:2, 30; 3:17; 5:11; 6:11,

15-20; 10:8). The words mean "set apart" for God's just purposes, not for cultural imitation. Family or household language abounds, with "brothers and sisters" used about thirty times (1:10-11, 26, and so forth). He appeals to them to consider not their own advantage but each other's good (6:12; 8:7-13; 10:23-24), to forgo their rights as he has (chap. 9), and to be a unified though diverse body marked by mutual benefit, not hierarchy and domination (12:12-26).

Paul's urging of cultural distance and distinctiveness (though not separation) is at odds with the imitation of imperial society that seems to be to the fore among some Corinthian believers, especially elite members. We do not know if the Corinthians, especially the elite, listened to Paul. But the situation that he addressed in the 50s indicated different believers negotiated their imperial society in different ways.

Philippi

The situation in Philippi seems to be closer to Thessalonica than to Corinth. Philippi was a small city, with about 9,000 to 12,000 people, and the church was probably small. Since Philippi was a colony (settled by Roman citizens), there were probably some Roman citizens in the congregation, but there is no evidence of elite members. Probably most members were artisans.

In verses 1:27-30 Paul refers to conflict and struggle. They have opponents; they suffer for Christ's sake; their conflict is the same as the imprisoned Paul's (1:7); their opponents will be destroyed. The link to Paul's suffering suggests not just general opposition to preaching, but civic conflict and opposition from imperial officials (1:12-13). As with Thessalonica, the most likely scenario is that converts have abandoned the idols of their previous Greco-Roman gods and withdrawn from imperial cult celebrations. These actions have caused fear among acquaintances, fellow workers, and kin alarmed by the possibility of reprisal from angered gods and of disaster for their community. The opposition probably involves local pressure—economic sanctions, verbal abuse, broken relationships, and perhaps occasional acts of violence. Local governing officials will also be involved if some Christians have refused oaths of loyalty to the emperor (as at Thessalonica).

The Philippians seem to have responded in several ways. Paul urges them in 1:27-28 to "stand firm," be united, and not be intimidated. The commands are only necessary if the Philippians have responded with wavering, disunity, and fear. Disunity is evident in at least three different responses to the situation of civic conflict.

To those who are afraid, Paul urges them to see their suffering as a participation in Christ's suffering and to remain steadfast (1:29; 2:8; 3:10-11). Others seem tempted to take on some signs of Jewish identity, whether from faithfulness to the scriptures, admiration for Judaism, or exemption from cult participation without civic conflict (3:2-11). Paul offers himself as one who has renounced any reliance on status in favor of knowing "Christ and the power of his resurrection and the sharing of his sufferings" (3:10). A third response involves those who continue to participate in cult observances, perhaps as part of collegia or artisan gatherings. The language and contrasts of 3:17-21 indicate that Paul attacks idolatry, gluttony, and illicit sexual activity. This cluster of themes was stereotypically associated with attacks on collegia gatherings. These believers perhaps saw no incompatibility between their Christian understandings and conventional cultural behaviors. Paul's strong language labels them "enemies of the cross," and contrasts their citizenship of the Roman Empire with their heavenly citizenship and savior-emperor, Jesus.

Paul's approach to their situation is to reject options two and three, and to support option one. He does not try to reduce the tensions and conflicts with their community. Rather, he exhorts them to continue to bear the suffering faithfully, as he and Christ did (1:2-26, 29; 2:17-18; 3:1; 4:4-9). He presents Jesus as a martyr, faithful and obedient even to death, but vindicated by God (2:6-11). In 2:4, support for one another involves economic assistance. Paul attempts to strengthen their community identity and boundaries as "brothers and sisters" (1:12; 3:1, 13, 17; 4:1, 8). He also uses military language; they are to be a united and faithful army (1:27).

Underlining Paul's approach is his conviction that God's sovereignty triumphs over Rome. His arrest cannot prevent the gospel from being spread through the Praetorian guard (1:12-14). There are believers even in the emperor's household (4:22). In 2:9-11 he presents the risen, exalted Jesus as having all authority "in heaven and on earth," including over Rome. On "the day of Christ" (1:10; 2:16), Jesus will finally enact that authority when he triumphantly returns from heaven (3:20).

This confidence in God's sovereignty gives rise to the most radical part of Paul's response, namely recontextualizing their citizenship. Using cognate words, he twice underscores that their citizenship is in heaven. In 1:27 they are to live as citizens of the gospel; in 3:20 they are citizens of heaven. This does not spiritualize their citizenship. Rather this language of citizenship denotes an everyday living of appropriate values, practices, and commitments to the Roman Empire. Paul wants the gospel to shape their living. In 3:20 he contrasts imperial citizenship with heavenly citizenship, and contrasts Jesus as Lord and savior with the Roman emperor, who was also known by these titles. Paul is calling for an alternative loyalty that is conflictual and treasonous. In effect, he is asking those who are Roman citizens to renounce that status, just as Christ renounced his status and became a slave (2:5-11). He is asking them to live as slaves as he and Timothy are "servants [slaves] of Christ Jesus" (1:1). Slaves were of course the lowest members of imperial society with few rights or privileges.

Paul's response here does not reduce their conflicts (as in Thessalonica), but ensures that they continue, if not escalate. Hence he exhorts them to be steadfast, faithful, and unified in their endurance until Jesus returns to complete God's purposes (3:20). He asserts that in the end, God's sovereignty over Rome's empire is sure.

The Cities of Revelation

Significantly, the New Testament story concludes in the book of Revelation with a vision of two cities, the whore Babylon and the new Jerusalem (chaps. 17–22). Revelation addresses Christians in seven cities and their surrounding areas in the province of Asia: Ephesus, Smyrna, Pergamum, Thyatira, Sardis, Philadelphia, and Laodicea (chaps. 2–3). A central issue for the author involves how Christians negotiate the complexities of political, economic, social, and religious life in these cities in Rome's empire. The writer is concerned that they have been too accommodated to the empire and wants them to be much more detached and distant.

The writing reveals the devilish nature of Rome's empire, which it identifies with the name of a previous great empire, the city of Babylon. Babylon's evils are numerous. In a regrettable negative female image, it is called a "great whore" (17:1). The image has a long biblical history (Exod. 34:15-16). It denotes faithlessness to God's purposes through cultural accommodation and compromise (22:14-15). The city of Babylon is faithless to God's purposes, blasphemously ignoring them (17:3). It is greedy and economically exploitative (17:4; chap. 18; see chapter 6, below). It is violent and murderous, destroying those faithful to God (17:6; 18:24). It is arrogant, "glorifying herself" and claiming to rule the world (18:7). It is under judgment (chaps. 17–18).

Accordingly, Revelation calls believers to "come out" of the whore Babylon so that they "do not take part in her sins" (18:4). The call is to refuse to participate in its civic, political, economic, and religious life. They are to resist and to live an alternative existence.

They are to live in the new Jerusalem. The two cities coexist, with the new Jerusalem situated in the midst of Babylon's evil (22:14-15). The two contrast greatly: whore and bride (19:7); beast (17:3) and lamb (21:9); demons (18:2) and God (21:3); fruitless (18:14) and fruitful (22:2); intoxicated (18:3) and healed (22:2); murderous (18:24) and free from death (21:4). The new Jerusalem is God's gift from "heaven" (21:2). It is where God and people live together (21:3). It is free from suffering, pain, and death (21:4). It transforms all that is contrary to God's purposes (21:5). It is huge, with plenty of room for everyone and outdoing any known city (12,000 stadia long equals about 1,500 miles; 21:16). It does not have a temple (21:22; see chapter 5, below, on temples). Interestingly, it embraces both city and countryside since it includes, in echoes of the Garden of Eden, a river and tree that produce a continual supply of life (22:1-2; see chapter 6, below). This is God's alternative to Rome's empire.

Conclusion

In this chapter we have seen some different ways in which Christians negotiated Rome's empire in their towns and countryside. Considerable diversity is evident in these responses. Paul's voice is loud in offering direction, as is the writer of Revelation. However, we do not know how many Christians in communities like Thessalonica, Corinth, Philippi, and the cities of Asia agreed with them or preferred other ways of negotiation.

CHAPTER 5

Temples and "Religious"/Political Personnel

For twenty-first-century people, words like *temple* and *priest* suggest religious places and personnel separate from politics and economics. That separation was not true for the first century and is not helpful for reading the New Testament. Religion was much more public, civic, and political. That did not make worship any less genuine. Rather, it recognized that religious places and personnel were embedded in the political-economic structures of the Roman imperial world. Although temples conducted worship, they also often provided religious or divine sanction for the political order and were instruments of elite economic and societal control. Whereas some were priests by descent, members of the elite in cities across the empire assumed priestly roles for periods of time as part of their civic involvement, providing political, economic, and societal leadership through managing temples and leading or sponsoring celebrations. These realities present another dimension of early Christian negotiation of Rome's world.

In this chapter, we will explore this interweaving of religion, politics, economics, and societal order by considering Jesus' conflict with the Jerusalem temple, Paul's dispute with the cult of Artemis in Ephesus, and the role of the imperial cult and honoring the emperor in 1 Peter and Revelation.

64

The Jerusalem Temple

The temple occupied a central place in Judean life as a center for worship and of national identity. Temple worship involved daily sacrifices, prayer (Acts 3:1), and perhaps readings and teaching from Torah (Luke 2:41-52; 19:1; 20:1; John 18:20). Additional sacrifices were offered on Sabbaths and festivals such as the Day of Atonement and the three great pilgrim festivals of Passover, Booths, and Weeks, along with private sacrifices. Priests comprised upper-level chief priests and lower-ranked priests. To be a priest or Levite required descent from a priestly or Levite family. The high-priestly families supervised personnel responsible for the temple's worship (priests, Levites); economics (provisioning the temple, administering funds); administration; and order (temple police, Acts 5:22; maintaining buildings). Lower-ranked priests like Zechariah traveled to Jerusalem from rural villages periodically to serve in the temple (Luke 1:8).

From its beginning, the Jerusalem temple was deeply embedded in the politics, economics, and societal structures of its world. When King Solomon built the first temple in the tenth century BCE, he used taxes to purchase supplies (1 Kings 4:7-28; 5:1-11; levied in kind), and he conscripted labor (1 Kings 5:13-18). Solomon claims a divinely sanctioned link between his kingly power and the temple built strategically on the sacred Mount Zion (1 Kings 8:14-26; 9:1-5; also 2 Sam. 7).

When the Babylonians captured Jerusalem in 587 BCE, they destroyed the temple. In 539, the Persian king, Cyrus, allowed the exiles to return home and ordered the rebuilding of the temple (Ezra 1:1-4; 6:1-12). When rebuilding was delayed, the prophet Haggai successfully advocated for it (Hag. 1:12). After its dedication in about 515 BCE (Ezra 6:8, 15), power was centered in the hands of a priest, Ezra, and other priestly families (Ezra 7–10).

Around the year 20 BCE, King Herod, puppet king of the Jews at Rome's instigation, enlarged and rebuilt this temple as part of his impoverishing and harsh rule (Josephus, *Ant.* 15.380-425; 16.154; 17.304-8). The Jewish historian Josephus attributes Herod's action not to religious devotion but to ambition for public honor and "eternal remembrance" (*Ant.* 15.380; 16.153, 157). Employing some 18,000 men (Josephus, *Ant.* 20.219), the temple construction had extensive economic implications. It was finished in the early 60s CE just before Jerusalem and the temple were destroyed by Rome in 70 CE. Josephus and Matthew see this military-political destruction as God's punishment, though for different reasons. Josephus, a priest, sees it as the penalty for revolt (*JW* 5.559; 6.409-12; 7.358-60), whereas Matthew regrettably views it as punishment for rejecting Jesus (Matt. 22:7).

High-priestly families controlled the temple's daily operations. Powerful, wealthy, and privileged, these elite leaders were "entrusted with the leadership of the nation" (Josephus, *Ant.* 20.251). Their temple base supplied divine sanction for their societal power. They and the temple had an ambivalent interaction with Rome. They were entrusted with faithfully overseeing the temple's vibrant worship practices that celebrated Israel's distinctive covenant relationship with God. In recalling liberation from Egypt, for instance, the Passover festival sustained hopes of freedom from oppressive rule. Josephus notes that it was on "festive occasions that sedition is most apt to break out" (*JW* 1.88), a point not lost on Roman governors who stationed troops in Jerusalem to maintain order during festivals (*JW* 5.244).

Yet the temple leaders also had to accommodate Roman demands for loyalty and cooperation. Rome did not require local people to abandon their religious practices. It did, however, draw local religious observance into supportive relationship with the empire and exert some control over it. Rome commonly ruled through mutually beneficial alliances with local elites who would maintain the Roman-dominated status quo. The Roman governor appointed the chief priest (Josephus, *Ant.* 18.33-35, 95). The Romans kept the chief-priestly garments in Jerusalem in the Antonia fortress, releasing them for festivals (Josephus, *Ant.* 15.403-8; 18.93-95). Sacrifices were offered in the temple *for* but not *to* the emperor and Rome (Josephus, *JW* 2.416).

When war against Rome seemed likely in 66 CE, the "chief priests and notables" and "the principal citizens ('powerful ones'), chief priests, and most notable Pharisees" try to prevent it (Josephus, *JW* 2.410-24; *Vita* 21). They quickly assure Rome of their loyalty, appeal to those advocating war to desist from a hopeless undertaking, and ask the Roman governor to intervene with troops. These actions demonstrate the pragmatism and ambivalent position of being Rome's allies.

Priests exercised and benefited from economic power. The temple required agricultural products: wood, oil, grain, spices, wine, salt, lambs, bulls, oxen, rams, and doves (*Letter of Aristeas* 92-95). These supplies came from priestly estates (Josephus, *Vita* 422), trade, and "first-fruit" tithes paid by peasant farmers in kind (Neh. 10:32-39). The temple was part slaughterhouse in offering sacrifices, part warehouse in storing supplies, and part bank with storage chambers for wealth (Josephus, *JW* 5.200; John 8:20). Various Roman officials—the governors Sabinus in 4 BCE, Pilate in the 20s, and Florus in the 60s—looted the wealth in the temple treasury (Josephus, *JW* 2.50, 175-77, 293).

Josephus notes that priests became rich from tithes and offerings (*Vita* 63); archaeological discoveries in Jerusalem confirm wealthy priestly dwellings. Jerusalem priests at times violently seized tithes even if poorer local priests starved (*Ant.* 20.181). The temple also collected a tax, which included those outside of Judea (Philo, *Spec. Leg.* 1.78; Josephus, *Ant.* 18.312). The emperor Vespasian co-opted this tax after 70 to rebuild the temple of Jupiter Capitolinus in Rome (Josephus, *JW* 7.218)! These taxes and tithes, plus those exacted by Rome and by local landowners, often amounted to perhaps 20 to 50 percent of a peasant farmer's yield. Indebtedness and expropriation of their land inevitably followed nonpayment.

Ambivalent attitudes to the temple among nonelites are evident. Peasants paid tithes; some made pilgrimages to Jerusalem for festivals, and some participated in an extraordinary defense of the temple. In 40 CE, the emperor Gaius Caligula ordered a statue of himself, as Zeus, installed in the temple. Many, including priests and other leaders, launched a sustained nonviolent protest. They abandoned their houses and fields to confront Petronius, the governor of Syria, declaring that they would die rather than see the temple violated (Philo, *Embassy* 222-42). Others seemed not so pleased with the temple. Through the 60s CE, "a rude peasant" called Jesus, son of Ananias, announced the temple's demise, only to be beaten by "some of the leading citizens" and by the Roman governor (Josephus, *JW* 6.300-309). When war began in 66, violent protests expressed hostility and resentment against the Rome-allied Jerusalem priestly leaders. Some nonelites attacked the high priest's house, killed him, and pursued "the notables and chief priests," burning the debt-record archives (Josephus, *JW* 2.426-29). To the consternation of Josephus and other priests, they ignored the elite priestly families to select by lot "ignoble and low born individuals" as new chief priests (Josephus, *JW* 4.147-61).

Jesus' Conflicts with Temple-Based Teaching

The Gospels present Jesus in conflict with this Jerusalem-based leadership. In Matthew 15:1, for example, he tangles with "Pharisees and scribes from Jerusalem," the city over which "chief priests and scribes"—allies with Herod and later Pilate—exercise power (16:21; 26:3, 57; 27:1-2). He tells parables against their leadership (Matt. 21:45). In John, "chief priests and Pharisees" send temple police to arrest Jesus (John 7:32-45; see also 11:47-53). Judas betrays Jesus to be arrested by soldiers (from the Roman governor) and "police from the chief priests and Pharisees" (18:3). Jesus' protest is not against the Torah since he quotes it and offers his own interpretations. Rather, his challenge is that their interpretations of Torah benefit the elite at the expense of the rest and that this injustice is disguised and sanctioned as God's will. He thereby confronts their societal structures and practices. For example:

- He protests their insistence that honoring the Sabbath means no work, a practice that could cause hardship and impoverishment for the majority poor. Citing David's eating of thanksgiving offerings in the temple reserved for priests, Jesus declares himself "greater than the temple" (12:6). He proposes instead honoring the Sabbath with good and merciful actions that repair the harm inflicted by the elite's system (Matt. 12:1-14).
- He protests their encouragement of people to make gifts to the temple that remove valuable resources from the elderly (Matt. 15:1-9). He declares that God does not legitimate the temple-based, Jerusalem-centered elite leadership (Matt. 15:13-14).
- He is less concerned with purity than with greedy, sinful actions that destroy human communities (Matt. 15:10-20).
- He condemns their emphases on tithing, external purity, and honoring past prophets, not because these practices are bad or unnecessary but because the leaders ignore justice, mercy, and faithfulness; practice extortion and greed; and do not receive

challenges to their system (Matt. 23:23-36). He announces that they and their temple system are under God's judgment (23:38).

Jesus' Conflicts with the Jerusalem Temple

Jesus' direct confrontation with the temple leaders emerges from this mixing of religion and politics, and from the considerable political, economic, societal, and religious power exercised by the temple leadership. In the synoptic Gospels, this confrontation occurs at the beginning of Jesus' last week when he enters Jerusalem (Mark 11:15-19; Matt. 21:12-17; Luke 19:45-48). It leads to his death, intensifying conflict that has pervaded each Gospel. In John, the incident occurs at the beginning of Jesus' ministry (2:13-22), framing the whole of Jesus' ministry as a conflict with this center of power.

Jesus drives out from the temple those who were buying and selling and the money changers. The former may be those who were buying the sacrifices they needed to offer, or they may be temple officials procuring supplies for the temple rituals. The money changers provided the acceptable temple currency of shekels and half-shekels for payment of the temple tax that funded temple operations. Both groups are the face of the enormous power of the temple. To attack these groups is not to cleanse the temple; it is to shut it down.

The Gospel narratives cast his action as an exorcism, thereby unfortunately demonizing the temple. The Gospels say that he "drove out" the sellers and the buyers (Mark 11:15; Matt. 21:12; Luke 19:45; John 2:15). The synoptic Gospels use this same verb "drove out" to describe Jesus casting out demons. The verb presents the temple as demonic and Jesus' action as an exorcism. With all its political, economic, societal, and religious power that benefits the ruling elite at the expense of the rest, the temple is in the control of the devil, the one who controls all the empires of the world (Matt. 4:8; Luke 4:5-6).

Jesus goes on to condemn the temple as a "den for robbers" instead of being "a house for prayer." The first phrase comes from Jeremiah's famous sermon condemning the king and temple leadership for oppressing the people (Jer. 7:11). Jeremiah speaks against those, especially the leaders, who act unjustly; oppress the alien, the orphan, and the widow; who shed innocent blood; steal;

69

murder; commit adultery; swear falsely; and worship other gods (7:5-9). He condemns them and their temple economy as robbers who steal the people's possessions and life. Jesus uses Jeremiah's phrase to condemn the temple system of his own day, presided over by the Roman-allied elite, including the chief priests.

But the term "robber" can also be translated "bandit." In the time of Jesus there were a number of peasant-based groups of bandits. Experiencing increasing economic and social hardship, they claimed power under the leadership of a charismatic figure to plunder elite property and attack elite personnel. In a sharp reversal of roles, Jesus applies the term "bandit" to the Jerusalem leaders to charge them with robbing the people and destroying and pillaging the nation!

As an alternative, Jesus sees the temple as a house of prayer. Jesus quotes from Isaiah 56:7 where the prophet envisions an inclusive people and temple embracing marginal persons such as eunuchs (cf. Lev. 21:16-23; Deut. 23:1) and foreigners. Jesus evokes this vision of welcome and merciful inclusion that describes his whole ministry. He has claimed to mediate God's forgiveness, healing wholeness, and social inclusion independently of the temple elite's attempts to control these blessings. In Matthew's account (Matt. 21:14), Jesus heals the blind and the lame, mediating God's transforming presence to those that the elite had previously excluded from the temple (Lev. 21:16-24; 2 Sam. 5:8).

The temple leadership perceives Jesus' actions and words in the temple as a rejection of their authority and temple system, and as offering a dangerous vision of alternative political, economic, and societal structures. In each Gospel, references to their attempts to kill Jesus or to his death follow immediately (Matt. 21:15, 23, 45-46; Mark 11:18; Luke 19:47; John 2:18-22). They have too much to lose to tolerate such a challenge.

Early Christians and the Temple

Whereas Luke's Gospel incorporates Jesus' condemnation of the Jerusalem temple (19:45-48), Luke-Acts as a whole is somewhat ambivalent about the temple (a full discussion is not possible here). At least in the initial chapters of both the Gospel and Acts, positive encounters happen in the temple. As conflict increases in Acts, followers of Jesus focus more on households.

70

Luke's Gospel begins with Zechariah undertaking his priestly duties in the temple. While doing so, an angel interrupts the temple liturgy to announce to him Elizabeth's conception of a son to be named John (1:5-23). The temple is a place of revelation. The Gospel ends with the disciples, who after encountering the risen Jesus and witnessing his ascension obediently return to Jerusalem. There they were "continually in the temple blessing God" (24:53). The temple is a place of worship.

The opening chapters of Acts alternate scenes that locate the disciples in households and in the temple. In households they assemble, pray, choose another leader, receive the spirit, preach, welcome new converts, learn, share all things, break bread, and experience persecution (1:12–2:47; 4:23–5:11; 6:1-11; 8:3). They also frequent the temple (2:46), but increasingly experience conflict with the temple leaders. A healing and preaching about the risen Jesus (chap. 3), including the accusation that the leaders had killed Jesus (3:15), provoke the wrath of the temple leaders with imprisonment (4:3) and threats (4:21). Further healings and preaching lead to imprisonment and floggings (5:12-42). Stephen preaches against the temple and proclaims its destruction (6:13-14). The temple leaders stone him to death (7:59). Thereafter, the followers of Jesus generally have little to do with the temple but household gatherings become more important. Later, Paul is accused of preaching against and violating the temple (21:28-40). The consequences, narrated in chapters 21 through 28, show how deeply the temple is embedded in the Roman political system. The temple leaders ally with Roman officials to defend their common interests and the hierarchical status quo against a possible threat. These conflicts show the leaders to be opposed to preaching about Jesus as God's messenger, to healings as signs of God's purposes for life and wholeness, and to any threat to their power and the temple's hold on people's lives.

Paul, Ephesus, and the Goddess Artemis (Acts 19:23-41)

Rome did not insist that those within the empire convert to Roman gods. Rome tolerated local religious observances and fused Roman gods with local gods as long as loyalty to Rome was secured. For the Jerusalem temple, for instance, Rome exercised control through its allies, the chief priests, who agreed to sacrifice two lambs and a bull twice daily *for* Rome and *for* the emperor's well-being, but not *to* the emperor. The refusal by lower-ranked priests to offer these sacrifices in 66 CE, despite the chief priests' protests, was understood to be rebellion and contributed to the outbreak of war (Josephus, *JW* 2.197, 409-10).

Accordingly, in Ephesus, capital of the Roman province of Asia and an important center for the early Christian movement, Rome did not resist the long-established and dominant worship of the goddess Artemis but ensured it was within Roman control. When Paul and other preachers of "the Way" in Ephesus encountered devotees of Artemis, they had to negotiate it not only as a religious phenomenon, but also as a central civic and imperial entity.

Artemis was a mother and/or wife goddess who was often represented in statues with what seem to be many breasts. People of Ephesus regarded this mother goddess as the divine protector and sustainer of civic life in the city. She was understood to have saved the city. Her temple, the Artemisium, impressive in size and wealth and one of the seven wonders of the ancient world, visually displayed her importance and the high regard in which she was held. Not surprisingly, a number of inscriptions and coins from Ephesus show emperors often linking themselves with the temple.

The temple of Artemis played an important role in the province's religious and civic life. The name Artemis was understood to derive from a Greek word meaning safe and happy. She was understood to be a merciful and benevolent goddess who satisfied people's needs. Through the temple personnel, she had power to give oracles and to intervene to improve situations. She was also understood to save people powerfully from cruel and indiscriminate cosmic powers. Preaching about Jesus rivaled such claims.

The temple played a crucial role in the province's economic life. Those who came to Ephesus to admire the temple's magnificence or to seek the goddess's intervention required food, shelter, and offerings. Because it was understood to be a divinely secured location, the temple provided facilities for people to deposit wealth. The temple gained further wealth from the production of the temple's large estates, sacred ponds, and herds. People left bequests to the temple in wills. Those who had sought the goddess's benefits made sacrifices, and those who had experienced her benefits made donations. Accordingly the elite overseers of the temple had substantial wealth from which to make extensive loans. Could a follower of Jesus take such a loan?

In addition to this economic involvement, the temple was important for the city's civic and legal life. Inscriptions attesting decisions made by the city council were deposited in the temple. The use of the temple as an archive suggested the goddess's sanction for the elite-controlled administration of the city. The temple was also an asylum for those in political danger, for debtors, for fugitives, and those needing assistance for any reason. It is important to remember that elite figures and groups were responsible for the administration of religious, economic, civic, and legal matters. They fostered, and benefited from, Artemis's power and status.

While Ephesus benefited from Artemis's presence, the city, notably its elite, understood itself to be responsible for the temple's administration and to be entrusted with the task of honoring the goddess (Acts 19:35). It did so in several ways. There were important annual festivals, one that celebrated Artemis's birth and one that celebrated her various roles. These festivals involved street parties, feasting, processions, and special cultic celebrations.

There is also evidence of a procession every two weeks along a route from the temple outside the city into the city to its theater. The procession carried numerous statues of Artemis, and involved more than 250 people. Elite persons played crucial roles in funding, organizing, and executing these celebrations, providing entertainment, food, and personnel. Through involvement in these civic responsibilities they gained social honor and power.

The silversmiths mentioned in Acts 19:24, who made silver shrines of Artemis, belong to this civic honoring of Artemis as protector of Ephesus. No such *silver* shrines have been discovered, but comparable items made of other materials existed as votive offerings. The loss of silver objects over several thousands of years is not surprising since it is a valuable metal.

The silversmiths in Acts 19 probably constitute a trade group or guild of silver workers. An inscription from Ephesus confirms the existence of such a group. Demetrius, their leader, may well be their elite patron who gains honor from funding and perhaps

73

hosting their monthly gatherings and protecting their interests. An inscription has been found that identifies a person named Demetrius on the board of wardens of Artemis's temple. However, the name Demetrius appears in numerous inscriptions so it may not be this particular Demetrius. The silversmiths are concerned about the impact of Paul's two years of preaching (19:10), notably his claim that "gods made with hands are not gods" (19:26; compare his approach in Athens, Acts 17:22-34). Their concern is partly economic (19:24-27a). Their other concern centers on Artemis's honor; if Christian preaching successfully takes people away from honoring Artemis, her role in Ephesus will be diminished, she will be offended (19:27b), and tragedy might befall the city. That is, the special relationship between Ephesus and Artemis would be destroyed and Artemis's role in providing divine protection and sustenance for Ephesians lost.

These concerns provoke cries of loyalty to Artemis (19:28), civic confusion, and a spontaneous gathering in the theater. They seize some of Paul's companions but not Paul (19:29-31). Further confusion and shouts of loyalty to Artemis follow (19:32-34), requiring the town clerk to assure the assembled crowd that the relationship between Artemis and Ephesus, the keeper or warden of Artemis's temple, is divinely secured and impregnable (19:35). He reminds them that there are recognized legal processes under Roman supervision for complaints (19:36-40). He dismisses the assembly and folk apparently leave peaceably, assured of Artemis's durability (19:41).

A number of clues indicates how deeply embedded is this scene in Roman imperial realities. As I have noted, the focus on Artemis, her temple, and all the activities associated with it implies numerous key roles for elite members of Ephesian society. The prevailing mind-set of civic responsibility encouraged acts of euergetism ("civic good works") or social benefaction in which elites involved themselves in civic roles and in funding activities in order to enhance their own status and power. Such actions expressed loyalty to and sought favor from Roman officials, who rewarded leading citizens with further opportunities to enhance their wealth, honor, and power.

It seems from verse 31 of Acts 19 that Paul has befriended some of the elite, officeholders called Asiarchs. This title refers to a variety of functions within the city's administration carried out by elite members; some functions associated with the powerful city council and some involving duties associated with the temple. No information clarifies how Paul had contact with these Asiarchs, and some interpreters think it is historically unlikely that Paul would have had such contact. But the narrative causes us to wonder how he might have met them. Perhaps they had heard him preach in the hall of Tyrannus (Acts 19:9). Some of them are described as being friends of Paul. The category of friendship indicates their obligation to Paul to keep him safe.

The town clerk plays a leading role in the scene. He is a powerful member of the elite, associated with the city council and often responsible for record keeping. His importance is also reflected in that he addresses, calms, and dismisses the crowd (19:35-41). He does these tasks not by advocating for Paul, as many interpreters have mistakenly claimed, but by rehearsing central civic affirmations, defending Artemis, and maintaining Roman control. This Rome-friendly elite Ephesian upholds Artemis's central role in the city and honors the great value Rome places on civic order. Artemis and Rome guarantee and protect elite control, which means elite wealth and power over the city. Accordingly he:

- Declares Ephesus's premiere role in being the keeper of Artemis's temple (19:35*a*). Ephesus's relationship with and role in honoring Artemis will not change at all.
- Reminds them of the sacred stone or statue that fell from heaven, a reference to a sign from Zeus that legitimated Artemis's power. It refutes Paul's claims that Artemis was made by human hands and is therefore not a god (19:26, 35*b*).
- Assures them that nothing can shake or contradict these bedrock affirmations (19:36*a*). The Demetrius-led civic disturbance is unnecessary (19:37). The town clerk does not think Christian preaching poses a threat.
- Indicates that Paul and his associates have not violated Artemis's temple as "temple robbers" or blasphemers (19:37).
- Reminds (and thereby rebukes) Demetrius and his crafts guild of recognized channels for expressing a complaint, namely the courts and the Roman proconsul (19:38), and the regular (rather than a spontaneous) assembly (19:39). Roman processes

75

protect Artemis. Ironically, Demetrius, not Paul, is the one charged with endangering civic order.

- Warns everybody of the great danger from the Romans of being perceived to have rioted (19:40). The town clerk, an elite ally of Rome charged with protecting the status quo, clearly seeks to prevent disorder and its consequences.

The town clerk has good reason to be concerned about Roman intervention, especially in relation to disturbances concerning Artemis. Twice in previous decades Rome had intervened. Concerned that the right to asylum at temples was being widely violated whereby runaway slaves, debtors, and criminals found unwarranted protection, the emperor Tiberius (14–37 CE) and the senate required cities, including Ephesus, to petition for the right to extend asylum at Artemis's temple. The right was renewed but notice was served that the Artemis temple needed to ensure it upheld rather than undermined public order (Tacitus, *Ann.* 3.60-63).

Also, around 44 CE the emperor Claudius and the proconsul Persicus addressed some corrupt financial dealings in the Artemis temple that had seriously reduced the temple's revenue. They issued decrees to prevent the situation recurring. Civic disorder would certainly bring further intervention.

Why does Acts tell this story? How does it help followers of Jesus negotiate the Roman Empire? Often, interpreters claim the story declares the Christian movement's victory over goddesses like Artemis and over Rome's elite allies. Preachers like Paul, so the argument goes, are protected from unruly mobs and defended by elite civic officials.

But such a reading is difficult to sustain and ignores the ways in which both Artemis and Rome exerted power over centers like Ephesus. Rather, the scene not only exposes fundamental conflicts between followers of Jesus and of Artemis, but also shows the difficulty and the threat of proclaiming the Christian message in such a context. Preaching can create opposition. Paul's preaching collides with civic claims and provokes Demetrius and a civic uproar. The scene does not indicate whether Demetrius pursues his complaints through the courts, proconsuls, or regular assembly. But given the gravity of his charges and the widespread support they elicit, it seems unlikely that the issue just goes away. Preachers need to be ready for a hostile response.

The conflict also silences preaching. Paul cannot reach the theater to address the crowd; the elite officials and friends dissuade him from attending (19:30-31). Gaius and Aristarchus do not get to speak (19:29). Alexander fares no better (19:33-34). Paul departs Ephesus soon after, leaving the believers to continue to negotiate life in the city on a daily basis (20:1). Perhaps they do so by not participating in anything to do with Artemis (15:19-20). But after Paul's unsuccessful attempt to confront the temple's activities directly, it seems unlikely that the scene encourages them to do so. Rather, they must live in this multireligious world, finding their own faithful place in it without necessarily expecting to overturn its civic and imperial structures.

Imperial Cult: 1 Peter and Revelation

1 Peter

Just as Rome did not forbid worship of local deities, whether in the Jerusalem temple or the temple of Artemis in Ephesus, it did not force people to worship the emperor. I noted above the accommodation with monotheism worked out for the Jerusalem temple. Rome did, however, increasingly encourage such public and communal worship, and elites in cities throughout the empire increasingly advocated it, partly to honor the emperor, partly to enhance the prestige of their own cities, and as another way in which they might enhance their own honor, status, and power. Although involvement in emperor worship was not compulsory, significant pressures were exerted on nonelites to participate.

The imperial cult expressed and created the relationship between ruler and ruled. It rendered the emperor visible to his subjects. The most visible expression involved temples in cities that were wardens or keepers of imperial temples. In the province of Asia, in 23 CE, for example, the emperor Tiberius permitted Smyrna rather than Ephesus to build an imperial temple, partly because of the latter's strong devotion to Artemis. But in 89 or 90 CE Ephesus was able to establish another temple for imperial worship. There were at least thirty-five "temple warden" cities in Asia Minor by the late first century. In addition to temples, statues of emperors might be located in baths, gymnasia, theaters, porticoes, and homes.

There were numerous opportunities for both elites and nonelites to participate in the imperial cult. Festivals had a central role in marking significant events such as an emperor's birthday, accession, military victories, and so forth. Festivals were multidimensional and offered numerous means for involvement, including processions through streets, prayers and hymns, oaths of loyalty, the offering of sacrifices (wine, cakes, incense, animals) at both central locations (council houses, squares, stadia, theaters, and so forth) as well as at small altars along the route. There were also street feasts, competitions, entertainments (gladiatorial displays, horseracing, animal fights, athletic contests), and distributions of food. Meetings of trade and artisan guilds or associations (silver workers, butchers, bakers, fish dealers, wool workers, and so forth) honored emperors at their regular gatherings by offering prayers, making sacrifices, and consuming meals involving food offered to gods. Imperial images were also located in households, especially elite households, where incense, sacrifices, and prayers were offered. In addition to public and temple monies, elites provided personnel and funding for many of these activities.

These festivals unified populations, the cultic calendar provided societal rhythm and organization, and cult sacrifices were a common source of meat sold in the restaurants often associated with temples. How did Christians, for example, in the provinces addressed by 1 Peter (Pontus, Galatia, Cappadocia, Asia, and Bithynia; 1 Pet. 1:1) and in the seven cities in Asia addressed in Revelation (Ephesus, Smyrna, Pergamum, Thyatira, Sardis, Philadelphia, and Laodicea; Rev. 2–3) negotiate these observances? What did they do on festival days? Did they join in the feasts? Did they watch the processions? Did they participate in guild meetings, which were crucial places for social interaction and building economic networks? Did they join in offering incense or cakes or wine to an imperial image, or did they go late and avoid the sacrifices?

These questions are difficult to answer. For example, 1 Peter instructs Christians to adopt behaviors that enable them to fit in with the norms of the rest of society. They are to "maintain good conduct among the Gentiles so that if they accuse you of wrongdoing they may see your good deeds and glorify God" (1 Peter 2:12, author's translation). They are to submit to human institutions (2:13) because God's will concerns their "doing right" (2:15). Slaves are to submit to their masters (2:18), wives to their husbands (3:1). As part of this very conventional behavior, they are to be subject to the emperor (2:13) and honor the emperor (2:17).

We have seen in the description above the "good conduct" of those who honored the emperor with sacrifices, festivals, feasts, competitions, and so forth. What did Christians do? Some interpreters have said that of course Christians would not be involved in offering sacrifices. But we cannot dismiss the possibility of idol worship too quickly. Some Christians in Corinth did not "shun idol worship," and Paul was willing to eat food offered to idols though others were not (1 Cor. 8–10). A decree sent out by the Jerusalem council forbids food offered to idols, but the prohibition would be unnecessary unless some Christians thought it acceptable to eat such food (Acts 15:28-29). The late-second-century Christian writer Tertullian, writing some one hundred years after 1 Peter, has to argue against Christians being involved in idolatry (*De Idol* 17.1). And the third-century Christian Origen knows Christians who bow before images, pretending to worship as was the social custom, but not doing so wholeheartedly (*In Exodum Homilia* 8.4).

First Peter's emphasis on "good conduct" and submission may suggest an expectation that Christians would be involved in imperial celebrations. If a master led his household in offering incense to a household image of the emperor, Christian slaves would obey the letter's teaching on submission by participating. So, too, would a Christian wife. In neither situation does the letter include an exceptive clause, "submit *except in* circumstances involving sacrifices." It is interesting that while the letter employs many citations from the Old Testament, not once does it quote a prohibition against idolatry. It does forbid participation in "lawless idolatry" (4:3-4) but the prohibition is part of a list forbidding immoderate or excessive behaviors. The letter does not forbid Christians from having sex, or drinking any wine, or associating with friends; but it does forbid socially disruptive, excessive, and reckless practices.

Moreover in 3:15, it exhorts believers to "in your hearts reverence Christ as Lord" (RSV). The heart is the center of a person's commitments and loyalties. To reverence Christ as Lord in one's innermost being is to recognize him as the one in whom

79

God's saving purposes are manifested. The heart is known only to God. Such an emphasis leaves open the possibility of assuming other roles, such as participating publicly in imperial cult celebrations and sacrifices as a social convention, without involving one's heart or innermost being. This is the practice noted by Origen (above) that some third-century Christians seem to have adopted as a way of coping with the expectations of their society while preserving their commitment to Christ. It could mean that Christians addressed by 1 Peter participated in honoring the emperor in street festivals or when incense was offered in a trade-guild meeting or household observance.

Revelation

Understanding what 1 Peter requires of its Christian readers may be both complicated and clarified by another document, the book of Revelation. Revelation addresses seven churches in Asia, part of the same area addressed by 1 Peter. Not only do their audiences overlap, but the two texts are written around the same time in the last few decades of the first century.

Revelation is, in part, a letter to all seven churches (see Rev. 1:4-5). But it includes within it letters specifically addressed to each church. These individual letters comprise chapters 2 and 3. Significantly, in perhaps four of the seven letters, the writer of Revelation acknowledges that some church members participate in idol worship and expresses strong opposition to the practice.

For example, in addressing the church in Ephesus, the stronghold of Artemis and location of an imperial temple (2:1-7), he notes that they "hate the works of the Nicolaitans, which I also hate" (2:6). Who are the Nicolaitans? In the letter to the church in Pergamum (2:12-17), also the site of an imperial temple, the writer strongly opposes those that "hold to the teaching of Balaam" to "eat food sacrificed to idols and practice fornication [immorality]" (2:14). "Immorality" may be a literal reference or it may be a common Hebrew Bible metaphor for idolatrous worship. Some in the church at Pergamum participate in worship of images, probably including images of the emperor. Verse 15 seems to sum up the previous verse by calling these people Nicolaitans. If this is correct, it clarifies the problem referred to in verse 6 in Ephesus. Some in the church in Ephesus also participate in worship involving idols. The next letter, to the church in Thyatira (2:18-29), refers to its tolerance of a teacher who advocates the same two practices, eating food offered to idols and immorality (2:20-23). It is also possible that the reference in 3:4-5 to the few in Sardis who have not soiled their garments may also refer to involvement in worship of images.

What is clear in these letters is that the churches in Asia are themselves divided over how to engage the empire. Some Christians take a very participationist and accommodationist approach, joining in imperial cultic activity. Others adopt much more distancing practices, probably involving some social and economic hardship. The writer of Revelation clearly supports the latter approach and condemns the former. He is adamant that there can be no compromise, no involvement in idol worship. One of the revelations of this book is that the empire is evil and under the power of the devil. Participation in the imperial cult means not just worship of the emperor but worship of the devil (chap. 13). The empire's political and economic life is under God's judgment (chap. 18). Interestingly, when this evil Roman imperial world is judged and destroyed by God, and when God's life-giving and just purposes are established in a "new heaven and a new earth" and in the new Jerusalem (21:1-21), there will be no temple in the city (21:22). With the end of the imperial world, there is no need for temples that are deeply embedded in political, social, economic, and religious systems that constitute the empire.

One of the implications of Revelation's analysis is that believers must distance themselves from any civic festivals, guild meetings, and household observances of imperial worship. But this approach is of course directly in conflict with 1 Peter's instruction to "honor the emperor." Christians in Asia are being instructed to adopt two quite different strategies for negotiating the empire. They have to choose between two quite different sets of practices. Should they participate freely in the empire's life while reverencing Christ as Lord in their hearts? Or should they withdraw from its demonic social, political, economic, and religious structures? It is quite possible that the conflict evident in the churches addressed by Revelation involves some who follow 1 Peter's accommodationist teaching and those whose opposition is supported by Revelation itself.

Conclusion

In the Roman world, religion was not a private matter. Rather, its observance was explicitly public, very communal, and quite political. Temples were not separate religious entities removed from the political, economic, and social world. The Jerusalem temple, the Artemis temple in Ephesus, and the multifaceted observance of the imperial cult in temples and cities across the empire were deeply embedded in Roman imperial structures. Christians were by no means in agreement on how to negotiate them. We have seen in this chapter a spectrum of responses embracing opposition, accommodation, and active participation.

CHAPTER 6

Imperial Theology:
A Clash of Theological and
Societal Claims

B y the first century, an important set of theological ideas was at work that expressed and legitimated Rome's empire and power.

- The gods have chosen Rome.
- Rome and its emperor are agents of the gods' rule, will, and presence among human beings.
- Rome manifests the gods' blessings—security, peace, justice, faithfulness, fertility—among those that submit to Rome's rule.

Rome and its elite allies in the empire's provinces actively promoted these claims. They expressed their understanding that Rome's dominating place in the world was the will of the gods. These ideas justified efforts to force people into submission to Rome. These ideas justified the empire's hierarchical society, the elite's self-enriching rule, and its privileged existence. These claims also promoted "appropriate" ways of living for inhabitants of the empire, notably submission and cooperation. To submit to Rome was to submit to the will of the gods, and the means of participating in their blessing. That is, these claims had profound implications for how society under Rome's control was structured, and how people lived.

Various "media" ensured that these expressions of and sanctions for Rome's rule circulated widely throughout the empire. Coins, the handheld billboards of the empire, proclaimed them in every marketplace with images of imperial figures and gods and goddesses. So did statues of imperial figures. Festivals announced them while celebrating the emperor's birthday or succession or military victory. Imperial and military personnel were the face of this divinely sanctioned empire and the agents of the gods' will. Archways or gates and imperial buildings declared them. Numerous writers, usually writing for literate elite audiences, repeated them.

The poet Virgil, for example, has Jupiter appoint Romulus to found Rome and its empire for which Jupiter declares, "I set no bounds in space or time; but have given empire without end" to Romans who will be "lords of the world" (*Aeneid* 1.254-82). Later Anchises announces to Aeneas that Rome's mission is "to rule the world...to crown peace with justice, to spare the vanquished, and to crush the proud" (*Aeneid* 6.851-53).

Around the time of Paul's mission, Seneca has the emperor Nero declare: "Have I of all mortals found favor with Heaven and been chosen to serve on earth as vicar of the gods? I am the arbiter of life and death for the nations" (*Clem.* 1.1.2). The Jewish historian Josephus has Rome's puppet Agrippa recognize that "without God's aid so vast an empire could never have been built up" (*JW* 2.390-91). Tacitus has a Roman governor remind the leader of a German tribe that "all men had to bow to the commands of their betters; it had been decreed by those gods whom they implored that with the Roman people should rest decisions what to give and what to take away" (Tacitus, *Ann.* 13.51).

Claims of Rome's election as the agent of the gods were made not only for the empire as a whole but also for specific emperors. Prior to Jesus' ministry, the emperor Augustus (31 BCE–14 CE) actively promoted these views, as did Vespasian, the emperor around the time that the Gospels were written. After much political instability in 68–69 CE, Vespasian emerges as the triumphant emperor. Suetonius notes various omens and signs that he claims indicate the gods' choice of and favor on Vespasian. One of these signs comprised a dream in which Nero was "to take the sacred chariot of Jupiter Optimus Maximus from its shrine to the house of Vespasian" (*Vespasian* 5.7). This dream was understood to signify the transfer of Jupiter's favor from the emperor Nero to

Vespasian as his divinely chosen successor. When Vespasian becomes emperor in 69 CE, the civil war of 68–69 ends and a year later his son Titus destroys Jerusalem and ends the rebellion in Judea. Vespasian issues coins that proclaim his coming to power as the work of several particular deities. Some coins depict Jupiter with a globe bestowing worldwide rule on Vespasian. Other coins prominently depict the goddesses peace (Pax) and victory (Victoria or Nike). These depictions present his reign as the will of the gods as well as announce particular divine blessings that he manifests among his subjects.

In referring to the emperor Domitian (81–96 CE) the poet Statius highlights his representative role as Jupiter's agent, declaring, "At Jupiter's command he [Domitian] rules for him the blessed world" (Statius, *Silvae* 4.3.128-29). And in referring to the emperor Trajan (98–117 CE), Pliny identifies the gods as "the guardians and defenders of our empire" and prays to Jupiter for "the safety of our prince" (*Pan.* 94).

This Roman imperial theology claimed that the gods through Rome's elite-controlled empire were sovereign over the world, had the right to direct it, and could determine what sort of human society, interactions, and behaviors should result. Compliance with Rome's rule was encouraged by presenting the empire's order as divinely sanctioned.

For followers of Jesus, these claims presented problems. Christians followed one whom the empire had crucified. Crucifixion was the empire's ultimate way of removing a person who challenged or threatened the empire. Christians understood Jesus to be Lord, not Jupiter. They understood that Jesus manifested the kingdom or reign or empire of God, not of Jupiter and Rome. How were they to negotiate this web of interlocking ideas, the empire and society they legitimated, and the daily behaviors and practices they shaped? We will look at three New Testament writers who contest and imitate these claims with alternative theological and societal visions.

Paul

As we saw in chapter 4, Paul addresses his letters to small communities of followers of Jesus in urban centers throughout the empire. These communities often struggled to determine appropriate interaction with their surrounding civic communities. How should they negotiate the claims about Rome's divinely sanctioned role? Should they participate in festivals that honored the emperor? What should their attitudes and practices be toward imperial officials, festivals, and propaganda?

Paul does not urge these Jesus communities to remove themselves from their cities or to turn their backs on civic affairs. He does not advocate escape from or dismissal of the political-civic-societal challenges of the empire. Nor does he urge them to employ violent tactics to overthrow the empire.

Rather, he helps them negotiate these civic settings and imperial claims so as to remain faithful to God's purposes for the world. By emphasizing their special identity in God's purposes that are not yet complete, he reinforces their group identity and boundaries as distinct from, yet as participants in their surrounding community. He also frames their present challenges in the larger cosmic context of participating in God's just purposes for the world that, while not yet complete, will ultimately be victorious. That is, Christians belong to God's empire (Rom. 14:17; Phil. 3:20).

Notions of covenant significantly influenced Paul's theological thinking. God was faithful to God's promises to Israel as God's people and to bless all of God's creation with life (2 Cor. 1:20). Moreover, Paul was an apocalyptic thinker who understood that God's purposes were not yet completed. At the imminent return of Jesus, God would end this world shaped by sin and death and establish God's good and life-giving purposes for all. Fundamental to these claims was the conviction that the sovereignty of the world belonged not to Jupiter and Rome but to God (Rom. 1:18-32; 11:33-36; 1 Cor. 8:6; 10:26 quoting Ps. 24:1, "The earth is the Lord's."). And God's universal and inclusive sovereignty was worked out in inclusive, ethnically mixed communities that provided communal experiences and practices alternative to the empire's elite-dominated, hierarchical, and exclusionary societal structures. Paul sees the gospel from and about God (Rom. 1:1) revealing God's sovereign purposes in Rome's world.

Paul's gospel and communities present a significant theological challenge to Rome's claims. Fundamental to his gospel is the claim that there is one God (Rom. 3:27), the creator of all (Rom. 1:18-32).

"There may be so-called gods in heaven or on earth—as in fact there are many gods and many lords—yet for us there is one God, the Father" (1 Cor. 8:6). Jupiter/Zeus was commonly called Father (Virgil, *Aeneid* 1.254, "the father of men and gods"), and the emperor was known as "Father of the Fatherland." He was seen as a father having authority over and blessing the members of his large (submissive) household that comprised his empire.

Over against these claims Paul draws on Hebrew Bible traditions to identify Israel's God as the father of believers (Deut. 32:6; Jer. 3:19-20; Rom. 1:1, 7b). In Galatians 4:8 he dismisses these "so-called gods" as "beings that by nature are not gods," and in Romans 8:38-39 declares that all cosmic powers are powerless in relation to God's loving, saving actions. For believers, there is "one Lord, Jesus Christ" (1 Cor. 8:6; Rom. 1:1). Again Paul uses language here that was commonly used for the emperor ("Lord"). Paul's constant use of language closely associated with imperial power, and his redefinition of these terms with Christian content, indicates a direct challenge to the gospel of Caesar.

Paul's attack not only dismisses polytheism, but also confronts Roman imperial theology, challenging the divine sanction for the empire. If there are no other gods, and only one divine Father, Rome's claims to rule and shape the world according to the sovereign will of Jupiter and the rest of the gods is exposed as empty. Christians could find here every reason for not participating in imperial rituals in houses, guild meetings, or civic festivals.

Further, Paul's analysis of the world reveals that the world under Rome's power is not ordered according to God's purposes. It does not recognize God's sovereignty. It ensures misplaced loyalties whereby people worship creatures not the creator (Rom. 1:18-32). Paul calls idols or images, which must include those of emperors, the dwelling place of demons (1 Cor. 10:20-21). Worship of idols expresses the failure to acknowledge God; this failure is accompanied by destructive social relationships (Rom. 1:29-31). This world is ruled over by powers hostile to God's purposes, namely sin and death (Rom. 6:9, 14); flesh (Rom. 8:7); and Satan (Rom. 16:20). This present age under Rome's rule (contrasted with the coming age of God's reign) is evil (Gal. 1:4). It is marked by "ungodliness and wickedness" (Rom. 1:18). Its wisdom is folly compared to God's ways (1 Cor. 2:6). This is a scathing condemnation of Rome's hierarchical, exploitative, and legionary empire.

God's intervention, though, is bringing this situation to an end (Rom. 16:20). Paul's view is clearly at odds with claims that the emperor had saved the world and instituted the golden age blessed by the gods. The notion of the golden age, the *saeculum aureum*, was especially associated with the emperor Augustus (died 14 CE). It referred to a social order marked by virtue and tranquility and achieved through war, triumph, and domination. During the 50s, the time of Paul, Seneca employs it in his work "On Mercy," written to instruct the emperor Nero (54–68 CE). Seneca presents Nero as the only hope to rescue the world from sinfulness through his "merciful" rule! Seneca does not imagine for one moment the collapse of Rome's empire but writes to uphold it. Paul has another agenda. God "the Father of mercies" (2 Cor. 1:3-4), not Rome, will faithfully bring life to all people (Eph. 2:4). God's empire and justice will save the world (Rom. 14:17).

God's agent in asserting God's sovereignty is Jesus. Paul focuses on Jesus' death, resurrection, and return. Jesus' faithfulness to God's purposes results in his crucifixion. Rome used crucifixion as a form of torture that removed threats to the imperial system and intimidated others into submissive compliance. Paul names "the rulers of this age" (1 Cor. 2:8) as those responsible for Jesus' death. The phrase has been interpreted to refer to either heavenly powers or human rulers. More likely it refers to both, designating the imperial agents and the supernatural powers at work behind the scenes. Paul's proclamation of "Christ crucified" (1 Cor. 1:23; 2:2) reveals the profound antipathy between God's purposes, expressed in Jesus, and the imperial world. Its rulers employ violence to protect their order and power against Jesus' threat. Jesus undergoes the fate of many enslaved by the emperor who dare to envisage a different order (Phil. 2:7).

Despite claims of "eternal Rome" that will rule its empire forever, the cross also reveals the limits of Roman power. Rome cannot keep Jesus dead. God gives "life to the dead" (Rom. 4:17). Jesus' resurrection anticipates the destruction of the ruling powers (1 Cor. 2:8), the general resurrection, and the establishment of God's empire over all (1 Cor. 15:20-28). God will end this unjust and idolatrous imperial system at the final "coming" of Jesus (1 Thess. 2:19; 3:13; 4:15; 5:23; 1 Cor. 15:23). Paul again takes an imperial term, *parousia,* which commonly referred to the arrival of an imperial official, general, or emperor (e.g., Josephus, *JW* 5.410, Titus), and applies it to Jesus and the establishment of God's purposes.

Paul identifies "the Lord Jesus Christ," who will come from heaven to accomplish these purposes, as the "savior" (Phil. 3:20). Again he uses a term "savior" (*sōtēr*) that was widely used for the emperor (Josephus, *JW* 3.459, *Vespasian*). By using it for Jesus, Paul indicates that he does not think Rome and its emperors have saved the world from anything. Rome's claim to have brought security and safety, to have effected deliverance from danger (*sōtēria*), is false. Rather God saves the world from Rome and its false claims. At Jesus' coming, in a vision that imitates imperial triumphs, "every ruler and every authority and power" are destroyed; "all his enemies" are put "under his feet" and subjected to God's reign (1 Cor. 15:23-28; Phil. 2:5-11).

This "coming" of Jesus (1 Thess. 4:15), this "day of the Lord" (5:2), will take place at an unknown time. Jesus will invade the Roman world where people declare "there is peace and security" (1 Thess. 5:3). This phrase openly evokes Rome's boast to have gifted the world with these blessings (Josephus, *JW* 6.345-46). The Pax Romana ("Roman peace") was celebrated, for example, on the Ara Pacis Augustae in Rome, the Altar of Augustan Peace. This cube-shaped monument, with highly decorated walls, witnessed to Rome's victories in wars that derived from its faithfulness to its god-given mission to rule the world. Faithfulness produced military victories, which produced peace. Peace meant submission to Rome enforced by military might or negotiated through treaties and alliances. "Peace" and "security" described a world under elite hierarchical control and ruled for the benefit of a few. Paul critiques this imperial world as "night" and "darkness" (1 Thess. 5:5). It is contrary to a world ordered according to God's just purposes for well-being (salvation) for all people.

In the time before Jesus' coming, Paul sees God at work in the midst of and over against Rome's world. He names God's working as "grace and peace" (1 Thess. 1:1). Grace is God's powerful free gift that creates peace, a world marked by wholeness and justice for all people. In the meantime, believers participate in God's purposes with lived faithfulness, love, and hope for God's imminent salvation from such a world, which will be accomplished at Jesus' coming (5:8-11).

In Romans, he declares that God is at work now, powerfully and faithfully, for salvation (Rom. 1:16-17). This is the gospel, the good news that reveals the justice or righteousness of God through God's faithfulness (1:16-17). Paul declares: "I am not ashamed of the gospel; it is the power of God for salvation to everyone who has faith [or faithfulness], to the Jew first and also to the Greek. For in it the righteousness [or justice] of God is revealed through faith for faith." These verses in the opening chapters of Romans sum up the letter's central claim. Significantly, the two verses are full of words that were commonly used imperial terms. Again Paul confronts imperial claims, denying their legitimacy by contrasting them with God's significantly different purposes of justice for all.

- *Good news:* This term often denoted the empire's benefits such as an emperor's birth, military conquest, or accession to power (Josephus, *JW* 4.618). In the tradition of Isaiah (especially Isa. 40 and 52), Paul uses the same language to speak not of Rome's so-called blessings but of God's saving activity and the establishment of God's reign or empire in place of Rome's (Isa. 52:7). To believe the gospel is to commit to and to be obedient to God as king or emperor (Rom. 1:5).
- *Salvation:* This term also named the blessings of Rome's world, especially its security and order achieved through deliverance from all threats and dangers. But this order, of course, was nothing other than benefit for a few—Rome's military power—and enforced submission for most. Again evoking the tradition of Isaiah, Paul presents an alternative reality in which God's saving power frees from imperial powers (Isa. 45:17; 46:13) and creates wholeness or well-being for all (49:6; 52:10).
- *Righteousness or Justice:* Paul's gospel is a challenge to Rome, and he uses the imperial-sounding language of victory to affirm God's inevitable triumph (1 Cor. 15:57). But at least one factor suggests Paul is not just imitating the empire. What God is doing is fundamentally different. Rome proclaimed its mission to give justice to the world "to crown peace with justice" (Virgil, *Aeneid* 6.851-53; *Acts of Augustus* 34). There was a temple in Rome to Iustitia, the goddess Justice understood to be at work through Rome. Roman justice, however, was inevitably an agent of its imperial system. It functioned to sustain the control of the elite over the rest by punishing and removing

90

threats (like Jesus) to its power. Paul sees the gospel, not Rome, as revealing the justice (or righteousness) of God. And this justice is not punitive, self-serving, benefiting only the elite. This justice comprises God acting rightly or faithfully to God's covenant purposes announced in the promise to Abraham to bless all the nations of the earth (Gen. 12:1-3). God's action in the world is to make things right for all people, "to the Jew first and also to the Greek." This work is under way in Jesus' death and resurrection in which, by raising Jesus, God overcomes Roman injustice. This "right-making," justice-bringing work will be completed at Jesus' return.

• *Faith/fullness:* God's actions involving salvation or justice or righteousness derive from God's faithfulness. They are expressed through the faithfulness of Jesus (Rom. 3:21-26) and encountered in human faithfulness (often translated "believing" or "faith") that embraces lived trust, commitment, loyalty, and obedience (Rom. 1:5). Paul uses language that was central to imperial claims. The goddess *Fides,* loyalty or faithfulness, was understood to be active through the empire's rulers. The emperor represented Rome's loyalty or faithfulness to treaties and alliances (*Acts of Augustus* 31-34). But such loyalty required a reciprocal loyalty comprising submission to Rome's will and cooperation with Rome's self-benefiting rule. Paul announces God's faithfulness to vastly different purposes (justice for all) and invites hearers of the gospel to entrust themselves to those purposes, loyally participating in God's justice-bringing work.

Paul sees this theological challenge to Roman claims taking societal shape. God's work, proclaimed through Paul's mission, shapes communities that embody a different identity and alternative practices as participants in God's purposes. The Philippian believers represent God's purposes on earth though their citizenship or "commonwealth" is in heaven. Whereas they belong to the abode of God from which Jesus will come, they live now as a colony of foreigners or resettled veterans in foreign territory. Paul commonly addresses the communities as *ekklēsia* (1 Cor. 1:2; Gal. 1:2; Philem. 2). The term echoes both the language of the Greek form of the Old Testament (the Septuagint) for the assembled people of God, as well as the citizen assembly of Greek-speaking cities in the eastern Roman Empire. The term presents Paul's churches as rival assemblies.

91

He also frequently uses household language to denote their identity and relationships. With God as their father, they are brothers and sisters (Rom. 12:1; 1 Cor. 1:10-11). They are to show "familial" love for one another (Rom. 12:10). These assemblies are to exhibit different social relationships, replacing the exploitative social and gender hierarchies of the empire with more egalitarian and caring relationships (Gal. 3:28). Meals are to represent these different relationships (1 Cor. 11:17-34) as does the alternative economic practice of the collection from Gentile churches for the poor in Jerusalem (1 Cor. 16:1-4; 2 Cor. 8–9; Rom. 15:25-33).

It should be noted, though, that as much as Paul outlines this ideological and social alternative and challenge to the empire, he is also deeply influenced by this world of empire. He imitates imperial concepts in his presentation of God's overwhelming power. He celebrates his ministry as always being led in triumph (2 Cor. 2:14). He employs his own "imperial" and patriarchal authority to demand loyalty and obedience from the churches (1 Cor. 4:15). He enjoys the patronage of those who support his ministry (Phoebe, Rom. 16:1-4). He declares that slavery does not matter (Gal. 3:28) but does not seem to work against it. He urges submission to Rome in the difficult passage from Romans 13:1-7 that we will discuss in chapter 8. Yet throughout he also announces God's judgment on Rome's empire, and God's alternative life-giving and just purposes. The communities are to live as participants in God's purposes as communities of resistance and solidarity with those oppressed by Rome's power until God establishes God's purposes at Jesus' return.

Gospels

Theologically and socially the Gospels also contest these claims that the gods have chosen Rome to manifest the gods' sovereignty, presence, agency, and blessings.

Matthew

Sovereignty

Matthew's Gospel asserts repeatedly that the world belongs not to Rome at Jupiter's behest, but to God. God's sovereign purposes are being asserted over Rome's.

Matthew's opening genealogy reviews Israel's history by highlighting three big events that reveal God's sovereign purposes (1:1-17). God promises Abraham that through him God will bless all the nations of the earth (Gen. 12:1-3). God promises to David a kingdom that will last forever (2 Sam. 7:14). But the third major event, the fall of Jerusalem and exiling of leaders to Babylon in 587 BCE, seems to put these purposes at risk. The loss of land, the destruction of Jerusalem, and the exiling of its leadership seem to be the end of any blessing for others, let alone of an eternal kingdom. Verses 12 through 16 indicate, however, that God's purposes continue with a surprising return from exile. Imperial power cannot divert or defeat God's work. In between these major events, God works through all sorts of characters—male and female, good kings and bad kings, Jews and Gentiles, the important and the marginal—to continue God's purposes in Jesus the Christ. Significantly, Rome is not included in this review.

God asserts sovereignty in the conception of Jesus through the Spirit (1:18-25). God commissions Jesus to manifest God's saving presence in a world of sins (1:21-23). Rome's empire does not order the world according to God's purposes. True to form, one of Rome's agents challenges God's work in chapter 2. King Herod, in power as Rome's puppet king, uses his allies, the Jerusalem-based leaders, and the magi from the east to attempt to kill Jesus as a threat to his rule. However, God protects Jesus by using angels and dreams to thwart Herod's efforts. Three times the chapter ironically notes Herod's death (2:15, 19, 20).

In 4:1-11, the devil challenges the outworking of God's purposes by testing Jesus. The heart of the temptations concerns whether Jesus will be loyal to God's purposes as God's son and agent (3:13-17), or whether he will obey the devil. In the third temptation (4:8-9), the devil offers Jesus "all the kingdoms [empires] of the world" if Jesus will obey the devil. This offer is a stunning assertion of the devil's sovereignty over the world and its empires. It reveals an alliance between the devil and Rome and unveils the devil as the power behind Rome's empire.

Several verses later, in Rome's devilish world, Jesus begins his public ministry with a counterassertion. He announces God's sovereignty with the words, "the kingdom [empire] of heaven has come near" (4:17). The word "kingdom" or "empire" (in Greek, *basileia*) is the same word the devil used in 4:8 and is a common word for Rome's empire. The phrase "kingdom [empire] of heaven" sums up Jesus' commission to manifest God's saving presence. The rest of the Gospel elaborates God's empire or saving presence in scenes that show the assertion of God's sovereignty over human lives in the calling of disciples (4:18-22; 9:9); over diseases (4:23-25; chaps. 8–9); the wind and sea (8:23-27); demons (8:28-34; 12:28); sin (9:2-8); death (9:18-26; chap. 28); and over the Jerusalem temple and Jesus' opponents, the ruling group allied with Rome (chaps. 21–22). Jesus' language asserts God's sovereignty as "Our Father in heaven" (6:9) and "Lord of heaven and earth" (11:25). He teaches disciples to pray for God's sovereignty to be established: "Your kingdom [empire] come. Your will be done, on earth as it is in heaven" (6:10). His resurrection asserts God's sovereignty over both death and Rome's power. Rome is not able to keep Jesus dead. The risen Jesus declares that he shares with God "all authority in heaven and on earth" (28:18).

The ultimate assertion of God's sovereignty comes when Jesus returns as Son of Man. In 24:27-31, his return echoes Daniel 7 where God destroys all empires and establishes God's never-ending empire. Jesus destroys Rome's army (the eagle, 24:28) and the cosmic deities that supposedly sanction Rome's empire (24:29). Judgment over all people (24:31; 13:39-42) assesses whether people have fed the hungry, clothed the naked, and cared for the sick and imprisoned (25:31-46). Attending to these tasks is how disciples are to live until God's sovereignty, not Rome's, is established over all. As much as Matthew uses this eschatological expectation to contest Rome's sovereignty, it should be noted that the Gospel imitates imperial ways in this scene with the violent and forced imposition of God's empire over all people.

Presence

Matthew's Gospel disputes the claim that Rome and the emperor manifest the presence of the gods. Rather it asserts that God's presence to save and rule the world is manifested by Jesus.

In three very strategic locations, the Gospel asserts God's presence is manifested in Jesus. In 1:22-23, Jesus' commission to save from sins is elaborated with a citation from Isaiah 7:14 (and Isa. 8:8, 10) that identifies Jesus as " 'Emmanuel,' which means 'God is with us.' " This opening statement frames the Gospel's whole narrative. All of Jesus' actions and words—his teaching, healings, feedings, meals, exorcisms, conflicts—manifest God's saving presence.

The citation from Isaiah 7:14 highlights another dimension. Isaiah 7 through 9 concerns a threat to the southern kingdom Judah from the northern kingdom Israel and its ally Syria. God offers King Ahaz and his people a sign of God's presence with them and of their salvation. The birth of a baby, the next generation, promises their deliverance from the imperialist threat. This future, though, requires their present trust in God. Evoking this story interprets the circumstances of Matthew's community. They, too, live with an imperial threat. The baby Jesus is a sign to them of God's presence with them and deliverance from that threat. They, too, must trust God to work out God's saving purposes.

The second explicit statement of God's presence manifested by Jesus occurs in the middle of the Gospel in 18:20. Jesus promises to be present with the community of disciples gathered for prayer. Significantly, this assurance comes as part of a chapter that is often called "the community discourse." In chapter 18, Jesus spells out the sort of community that disciples who are committed to God's empire constitute. This community welcomes and cares for the vulnerable and least (18:1-14), practices reconciliation (18:15-20), and extends forgiveness (18:21-35). These commitments to mercy, inclusion, service, and reconciliation differ greatly from the empire's commitments to domination, exploitation, self-enriching rule, and submission. Jesus' presence constitutes an alternative societal experience.

The third explicit statement of God's presence manifested by Jesus comes at the close of the Gospel (28:18-20). The risen Jesus sends his disciples in mission to the world under Rome's power. But unlike Rome's mission to dominate and subdue, disciples are to announce and enact God's life-giving purposes and presence revealed by Jesus. Jesus promises to be with them "always, to the end of the age." His presence guides them in their discipleship, but also anticipates the final establishment of God's purposes.

Agency

The Gospel challenges the imperial claim that the emperor and Rome are agents chosen to manifest the gods' sovereignty, will, and presence among humans. It presents Jesus as God's chosen agent, commissioned to enact God's saving presence and life-giving empire among humans.

As we have noted, the very name given to Jesus denotes his commissioning to be God's agent. The angel of the Lord instructs Joseph to name him "Jesus" because "he will save his people from their sins" (1:21). His name, used some one hundred and fifty times in the Gospel, constantly articulates his identity as agent of God's purposes.

The Gospel also employs various "titles" for Jesus that denote his identity as agent of God. The opening verse identifies him as "Christ" (1:1, 17). This term, the Hebrew form of which is *Messiah*, means to be "dripped on" or "anointed." Anointing with oil signified that a priest (Lev. 4:3, 5), king (Ps. 2:7), prophet (1 Kings 19:16), and even the Gentile ruler, the Persian Cyrus (Isa. 44:28; 45:1), were set aside or commissioned by God for special roles. Some, but by no means all, Jewish traditions expected various types of messiah figures. Some of these figures would be anointed or commissioned to free the people from Rome (Ps. Sol. 17; 4 Ezra 12:32-34) or to have a role in establishing God's empire (1 Enoch 46–48). By identifying Jesus as Christ, the Gospel denotes him to be God's chosen agent.

Other terms express a similar claim. The Gospel identifies Jesus as God's son (2:15; 3:17; 4:3, 6; 11:25-27; 16:16). For first-century Christians, this term denotes one who is in special relationship with God and is an agent of God's purposes and will. For example, in the Hebrew Bible, the term *son* denotes the king (Ps. 2:7), Israel (Hos. 11:1), and the wise person (Wisd. of Sol. 2), all of whom represent God's purposes. As God's son, Jesus is the agent of God's saving presence and empire (1:21-23; 4:17). He enacts God's will in his words and actions. Those who commit to Jesus continue this task of being agents of God's purposes (10:7-8; 28:19-20). They are called "sons" or "children" of God. They make peace, not based on military power, but on God's justice (5:9). They love and pray for their enemies and persecutors rather than destroy them (5:44-45), thereby embodying God's indiscriminate love for all people.

Blessing or Societal Well-Being

The empire claimed that as the agents of the gods' sovereignty, presence, and will they brought well-being or blessings of peace, fertility, harmony, security, safety, and so forth to the world. Matthew does not accept this elite view and exposes it as false.

96

Rather, it is God's work in the world through Jesus and his follow-ers that manifests God's blessing, namely God's empire (4:17; 5:3, 10), good news (4:23), and justice/righteousness (5:10, 20; 6:33). Like Paul, Matthew uses vocabulary often used in imperial claims.

The Gospel reveals the world under Rome's rule to be a desper-ate, not a blessed, place for most inhabitants. The Gospel is peo-pled with sick folk (4:23-24; chaps. 8–9). Jesus brings healing. Rome's world is peopled with folk under the control of demons (4:24; 8:28-34). Jesus' exorcisms bring deliverance. Rome's world is a hungry place. Disciples pray for daily bread (6:10). Twice Jesus heals and feeds large crowds, supplying them with abundant food (14:13-21; 15:29-39).

The Sermon on the Mount, the first teaching discourse in the Gospel, opens with Jesus' declaration of blessings that result from the establishment of God's empire (4:17; 5:3-12). The first beati-tude blesses the "poor in spirit." Matthew does not spiritualize the beatitudes and bless a "spiritual" condition. Rather, Jesus has just healed numerous sick people (4:24-25). Their sickness has ren-dered their already poor and desperate lives even more precari-ous. Poverty is never only a physical phenomenon; it destroys a person's very core. It eats away at their spirit. Jesus declares these "poor in spirit," the materially, literally physically poor that com-prised some 97 percent of Rome's world, blessed. Why are they blessed? God's empire is at work already to restore the world to God's just purposes, and these purposes will be established.

Similarly, in 5:5 Jesus blesses the meek. The meek are not to be understood as the wimps or the doormats. Rather Jesus quotes from Psalm 37 in which the meek are the literal poor who are exploited by the powerful and wealthy and deprived of their land. Jesus quotes the repeated promise of Psalm 37 that God can be trusted to restore to them land, the basic resource needed for survival. The beatitude anticipates the eschatological completion of God's purposes.

The beatitudes also express God's blessing on those who live according to God's purposes in the present. Those who hunger and thirst for justice, who are merciful, who are pure in heart, who make peace and pay the consequences in opposition experience God's favor. Their actions fundamentally oppose values and prac-tices of the empire. They participate in an alternative societal reality. In 20:25-26, Jesus contrasts this way of life based on mercy and service with that of the empire. In contrast to the "rulers of the Gentiles" and their "great ones [who] are tyrants," the community of disciples identifies itself with the powerless and vulnerable. As slaves they are to seek the good, not the goods, of others.

Like Paul, Matthew challenges Rome's claims theologically and envisions an alternative societal experience in which God's sovereignty, presence, and blessing are encountered now and in the future through Jesus, God's agent.

Luke

Whereas the focus has been on Paul and Matthew, I will briefly note one more example in which a Gospel contests aspects of Rome's claims for divine sanction.

The opening chapters of Luke's Gospel introduce Jesus in language that disputes Rome's claims. The angel announces to Mary Mary's conception of Jesus and God's commissioning of Jesus as agent of God's sovereignty. "The Lord God will give to him the throne of his ancestor David. He will reign over the house of Jacob forever, and of his kingdom there will be no end" (1:32-33). Contrary to Rome's claim of divinely sanctioned rule that lasts forever, Luke recalls the promise to David of a kingdom that lasts forever (2 Sam. 7). And contrary to Rome's harsh and exploitative rule, Luke recalls the tradition that David is an agent of God's merciful and just rule (Ps. 72). Different sovereignties, agencies, and understandings of societal well-being clash.

Mary continues the theme in her hymn of praise, commonly called the Magnificat. "My soul magnifies the Lord, and my spirit rejoices in God my Savior, for he has looked with favor on the lowliness of his servant.... He has scattered the proud in the thoughts of their hearts. He has brought down the powerful from their thrones, and lifted up the lowly; he has filled the hungry with good things, and sent the rich away empty" (Luke 1:46-56, selections). Mary's words celebrate God's overthrow of Rome's world.

Luke emphasizes the birth of Jesus in the world ruled by the emperor Augustus and the governor Quirinius of Syria (2:1-2). All inhabitants participate in a census, the basis by which Rome levied taxes and tribute (2:1-5). The angel announces to shepherds the birth of Jesus using language that, as we have discussed above, contests Rome's claims: "I am bringing you *good news* of

98

great joy *for all the people:* to you is born this day in the *city of David a Savior,* who is *the Messiah, the Lord"* (2:11, emphasis added). The announcement presents Jesus' birth, not the emperor's, as good news. Jesus, not the emperor, is Savior and Lord. Jesus, not the emperor, is the rightly anointed agent (Messiah) and king in the line of David, entrusted with representing God's purposes. And those purposes do not reserve blessing for the privileged, powerful, wealthy few, but extend it to all people.

As we noted in chapter 2, Jesus begins his public ministry in Luke's account by quoting Isaiah 61. With this quote he declares his ministry to be God-given and himself to be the agent of God's blessing that will transform Rome's world.

> The Spirit of the Lord is upon me, because he has anointed me to bring good news to the poor. He has sent me to proclaim release to the captives and recovery of sight to the blind, to let the oppressed go free, to proclaim the year of the Lord's favor. (4:18-19)

The language of "release" and "year of the Lord's favor" recalls Leviticus 25. This chapter announces a Jubilee year every fifty years in which slaves are freed, debts cancelled, and land returned to original owners. The Jubilee year was a mechanism for preventing a society from developing that was dominated by the wealthy and powerful. Rome's world is not God's will. Jesus announces that God's activity to save and transform this world is under way. Like Paul and Matthew, Luke offers a theological and societal challenge to Rome's claims.

Conclusion

Rome asserted divine sanction for its empire, claiming that the gods had chosen Rome to manifest the gods' sovereignty, presence, agency, and blessings on earth. New Testament writings dispute Rome's claims, asserting over against them that God's purposes will eventually hold sway over human affairs. Paul's Letters and Gospels like Matthew and Luke present Jesus as the agent of God's sovereignty, presence, will, and blessings in the present and future. Disciples of Jesus are to continue his role in the meantime.

CHAPTER 7

Economics, Food, and Health

Rome's empire influenced every aspect of a person's life. In this chapter, we will look at some ways the early Christians and New Testament writers negotiated three everyday issues: supporting themselves (economics), feeding themselves (food), and caring for themselves (sickness and healing).

Economics

Some 2 to 3 percent of the population possessed most of the empire's wealth. The overwhelming percentage of the empire's inhabitants lacked it and struggled constantly to sustain a subsistence-level existence. The struggle was cyclic. They knew times when there was enough (or even a little surplus) and frequent times when there was too little.

I observed in chapter 4 that the empire's wealth was based in land ownership. Elites controlled the production, distribution (trade), and consumption of its products. That is, the economy was embedded in and reflected the hierarchical and oligarchical sociopolitical structures of the empire. We also saw that the elite used taxes, rents, loans, interest, tribute, and trade to redistribute production from peasant farmers, artisans, and unskilled workers to themselves. The ruling few gained considerable wealth, enjoyed lavish lifestyles, and consumed much of the production. The majority's hard manual work sustained the excessive lifestyles of the few. That is, economic structures were exploitative and unjust.

Matthew

In this context of lack, how are people to live? Is wealth evil, something to be hoarded or something to be redistributed?

Matthew's Gospel, like numerous New Testament writings, warns about the dangers of wealth. While talking about the "exceeding justice" (5:20) that is to mark the life of disciples committed to God's empire, Matthew's Jesus urges disciples to share whatever possessions they have. They are to give to those who beg (the desperate, 5:42*a*), to those who want to borrow (the equally poor, 5:42*b*), and to those in need (6:1-4, like themselves). Jesus encapsulates this making available of their limited possessions to others in his subsequent instruction not to "store up" (acquire, value) possessions (6:19-21). This communal responsibility reflects hearts focused on "heavenly treasures," doing the will of God (6:19-23). It is the way of life for a people who have decided against serving mammon (property, possessions), but have enslaved themselves to God's just purposes (6:24). It is the sort of behavior that anticipates the full establishment of God's purposes (25:31-46).

These same issues are evident in Jesus' encounter with the young "rich man" (19:16-30). This unnamed man, one of the elite, has "many possessions" (19:22-23). He asks Jesus about "eternal life," a synonym for entering life (19:17), being perfect (19:21), entering the empire of heaven (19:23-24), and being saved (19:25). He wants to participate in God's purposes. In response to Jesus' questions about his social ethic, he declares that he has kept the commandments against murder, adultery, stealing, and bearing false witness, while honoring his parents and loving his neighbor (19:18-19).

His answer, though, reveals his commitments to wealth and not to God's justice. His "many possessions" indicate that this elite man has deprived others of what they need (stealing). He has not loved his neighbors.

Jesus offers him a program that, if followed, would dismantle the high-status world of the empire's powerful and wealthy (19:21). Jesus lays out a process of repentance that begins with

101

selling the man's possessions. Presumably the man's possessions include his land, slaves, house, and investment properties, markers of his status and power. Then he is to divest himself of his wealth by giving it to the poor, those lacking resources, despised and exploited by the elite. This is an act of restitution that reverses the transfer of wealth from nonelites to elites and anticipates the redistribution of resources that will happen when God's purposes are fully established (cf. 5:5). Then he is to join the community of followers of Jesus in new social relationships marked by shared resources.

But the man declines Jesus' invitation (19:22). He is one who, like the seed sown on rocky ground, prefers the "lure of wealth" (13:20-22). Imperial wealth, not God's empire, rules his heart (6:24). He upholds the imperial system.

By contrast, the disciples have left everything to follow Jesus (19:27). This is not a literal statement since its speaker, Peter, has a house and family (8:14-15). However, it does signify different priorities. Jesus promises reward in the redistribution of resources and reshaping of community that mark the full establishment of God's purposes (19:29).

James

The Letter of James addresses a community experiencing significant economic oppression in an unknown location. They are identified in 1:1 as "the twelve tribes in the Dispersion." If this address is taken literally, they might live anywhere outside Palestine. If it is taken metaphorically, it would refer to their marginal location vis-à-vis civic, political, and economic rights.

The community, committed to Jesus (2:1), comprises mostly poor nonelites. The letter refers to the lowly (1:9); widows and orphans (1:27); the poor (2:2, 5-6); women and men who live by alms (2:15); those who do business (5:13); rural laborers and harvesters (5:4); and small farmers (5:7). These folk suffer various injustices. Widows and orphans were vulnerable in an androcentric world that required male protection. The poor have dirty clothing and experience social prejudice (2:2-5). They are "dragged into court" (2:6). The verb "dragged" suggests physical or legal violence. Some, men and women, lack clothing and food (2:15). Rural laborers are not paid their wages (5:4).

102

The letter attributes this suffering not to deficiencies of character (i.e., laziness), ethnicity, or gender, but to their oppressors. The rich dress elegantly and display their wealth with fine adornment, rather than using it to assist the poor (2:2). They oppress the poor in court (2:6). They blaspheme the name of God or Jesus that identifies this community of the poor (2:7). The rich accumulate and consume wealth (5:1-3). These wealthy, powerful landowners deny rural laborers their wages (5:4). They live luxuriously and pleasurably (5:5). They condemn and murder the righteous poor (5:6), probably a reference to the effect of withholding wages and depriving a household of necessary resources. Their oppression is social, legal, and economic.

There are also "conflicts and disputes" among the group (4:1). It is not clear what the conflicts are over. They may be class-based between the poor and the rich, but it is not clear that the oppressive rich belong to the group. Perhaps the conflicts involve the poor and the not-quite-so-poor mentioned in 4:13-17. These latter folk have some business skills and opportunity for making money in other towns. The letter rebukes them for their presumption about the future (4:14), their lack of attention to the Lord's will (4:15), their arrogant boasting (4:16), and their failure to do the right thing, namely provide for those in need (4:17).

Or, the conflicts may arise within the oppressed poor. In 2:1-4, for example, some of the poor who seem to have internalized the practices of their society are rebuked for imitating its deferential behaviors and dishonoring their fellow poor. In 4:1-10 the letter's audience is rebuked for being "friends of the world" rather than friends of God. Friendship with the world opposes God's purposes and seems to comprise imitating or desiring cultural values and practices rather than God's alternative way of life. In 4:11-12 they are forbidden to speak evil against one another. They are to listen to one another, being slow to speak and slow to anger (1:19).

In response to their oppression and conflict, the letter seeks to sustain lives that are faithful to God's purposes.

(1) It assures them of God's preference for and presence with the poor (2:5). Rahab the prostitute is an example of a culturally marginal and despised person whom God vindicates (2:25; see Joshua 2). God has chosen the poor and has promised them

participation in God's empire (2:5). The current distress is not God's making (1:13). God will vindicate them when God's purposes are finally established (1:12; 5:7-8).

(2) Conversely, the letter assures the poor of the inevitable demise of the rich and powerful who are under God's judgment. God brings the rich low, for they disappear like a withered flower in scorching heat (1:10-11). As friends of the world, the rich are enemies of God (4:4). Future miseries, the end of their wealth, and destruction await them (5:1-6).

(3) In the meantime, the poor are to form a faithful community. Nineteen times the letter uses "brother and sister" language to secure their identity (1:2, 9, 16, 19; 2:1, 5, 14-15; 3:1, 10, 12; 4:11 [3 times]; 5:7, 9, 10, 12, 19). It calls them to "love [their] neighbor as [themselves]" (2:8) and to show mercy (2:13).

(4) This community is to be marked by perseverance (1:3-4, 12; 5:11). This perseverance is not passivity or resignation, even though major changes in the empire's political, legal, and economic structures are not forthcoming. Rather, it is a form of resistance in that it refuses to be broken down by the oppressive circumstances. In 1:4 this perseverance affects maturity or perfection in faith through participating in God's purposes in the present. In 1:12 it means future participation in God's life when God's just purposes are finally established. Endurance means trusting God to complete God's purposes (5:7-9). In 5:11 Job models endurance. Job refused to accept his suffering as normative, vigorously protesting it and demanding God's justice.

(5) The community is also to be marked by integrity. The writer urges them to consistency between their confessing and their living. They are to be hearers and doers of the word (1:22-24). In 2:1-7 the writer points out that their favoritism toward the rich is inconsistent with God's preference for the poor, and challenges them to consistency. Likewise, there should be consistency between their faith and their works (2:14-26), and between their faith and their words (3:2-12). Such integrity of speech removes the need for oaths (5:12).

(6) The community is to practice nonviolence toward their oppressors (5:6). Nonviolence does not mean ready compliance. The letter offers no instruction to obey rulers or submit to the wealthy and powerful. Instead of deference or retaliation, they are

exhorted to endurance (above) and peacemaking (3:18). As with Matthew's beatitude (cf. Matt. 5:9), peacemaking means living for the wholeness and well-being that result from God's purposes. Of course, such peace differs greatly from the Pax Romana ("Roman peace") from which the powerful wealthy benefit.

(7) The community is to pray in its suffering (5:13). They are to pray for the sick (5:14-15) and for one another (5:16), thereby securing their communal relations. Elijah provides an example of powerful and effective prayer causing God to withhold and supply rain for the harvest. Prayer, then, is another strategy against the wealthy's unjust hoarding of resources that cause some to not have enough to wear or to eat (3:15).

Revelation

In Revelation chapter 18, the announcement of the downfall of Rome's empire particularly emphasizes its economic oppression. How does this announcement address the churches in seven cities in the province of Asia (Rev. 2–3)?

The chapter begins with an angel declaring, "Fallen, fallen is Babylon the great!" (18:2). Naming Rome "Babylon" echoes the prophet Jeremiah's condemnation of the Babylonian Empire (Jer. 50–51). The choice of Babylon reminds readers that this previously dominant empire has passed from the world scene because of God's judgment. Rome will experience the same fate. Another prophet, Ezekiel, had also declared judgment on Tyre's vast trade and economic empire (Ezek. 26–28).

As I noted in chapter 4 above, Babylon/Rome is also identified as a whore (17:1, 5, 15, 16; 19:2). The image denotes faithless activity that benefits only Rome and corrupts others; "The kings of the earth have committed fornication with her" (18:3). The image of illicit sexual activity ("fornication") commonly appears in prophetic condemnations of people unfaithful to God's purposes. The use of these images for Rome's empire, and particularly its economic activity, presents it as self-benefiting, exploitative, harmful to others, and under God's judgment. The further references to Babylon/Rome as a "dwelling place of demons" (18:2) and of deceiving the nations by "[her] sorcery" identify it as demonic and bewitching (18:23).

Revelation locates Rome's illicit economic activity within the larger context of Rome's imperial rule secured by military power and religious practices. In chapter 13, Revelation describes Rome as a beast with "authority over every tribe and people and language and nation, and all the inhabitants of the earth will worship it" (13:7-8*a*). The imperial cult—discussed above in chapters 4 and 5—presents Roman political power as sanctioned by the gods and fosters submissive compliance. Moreover, another beast "causes all...to be marked on the right hand or the forehead, so that no one can buy or sell who does not have the mark" (13:16-17). Economic activity means participation in this political-military-religious power.

Chapter 18 emphasizes the same interconnections. Verse 7 connects economic extravagance ("she lived luxuriously") with the idolatrous self-glorification of religious observance ("she glorified herself") and the political control of an eternal empire ("I rule as a queen;...I will never see grief"). The chapter ends by making explicit in verse 24 the fourth dimension, the vicious military conquest on which the empire was founded: "And in you was found the blood of prophets and of saints, and of all who have been slaughtered on earth." Economic oppression is embedded in the empire's political-religious control and sustained by its military viciousness.

The chapter announces God's judgment on Rome with plagues, pestilence, mourning, famine, and fire (18:4-8). Judgment is the present activity of the Lord God who is "mighty," superior in power to Rome (18:8). This announcement of judgment brings forth three laments or funeral dirges from three groups who have vested and invested interests in maintaining Rome's oppressive status quo. They lament the loss of the source of their wealth.

The first lamenters are "the kings of the earth" (18:9-10). In Psalm 2 the "kings of the earth" resist God. The designation identifies Rome's allied rulers theologically as opponents of, but no match for, God's purposes. Rome commonly formed alliances with local elites such as client kings (see the discussion in chapter 3, above), as well as members of ruling classes in provinces and cities throughout the empire. These political and economic allies benefited from Rome's power. By committing "fornication" with the whore Babylon they acquired luxurious lifestyles. Their lament emphasizes Rome's great power ("great city"; "mighty city"), but in noting Rome's rapid demise ("in one hour") they ironically attest its weakness before God's powerful judgment.

106

The second lamenters are the merchants or traders (18:11-14, 15-17a). These are not members of the elite, though they have benefited greatly from the empire's power and economic reach (18:15a). Often elites participated in trade indirectly through investment and through supplying agrarian-derived products. Merchants played a crucial role in moving goods from the provinces to Rome, the center of the empire. Whereas "all roads lead to Rome," even more so did all ships. Shipping was less expensive than road transportation and it could carry greater quantities.

The first of their two laments focuses, self-centeredly, on the loss of Rome as a market: "No one buys their cargo anymore" (18:11). Verses 12 and 13 identify twenty-eight items brought to Rome from the provinces. Many of the listed items were expensive items that serviced the conspicuous consumption of excessive elite lifestyles. The list is wide-ranging, including highly valued decorative items (gold, silver, precious stones, pearls); textiles (fine linen, purple, silk, scarlet); scented or citrus wood (used especially for making expensive tables); items made from ivory and from costly wood; metals (bronze, iron); marble; spices (cinnamon, amomum, myrrh, frankincense); food items (wine, olive oil, wheat); animals (cattle, sheep, horses); transportation (chariots); and human slaves. Among the luxury goods are everyday items, especially those of food. By one estimate, Rome needed six thousand boatloads of grain per year to arrive at its port Ostia to keep Rome fed. Paul travels on one such boat from Alexandria in Acts 27:6.

But while the merchants lament the loss of a market, items on the list reveal Rome's exploitative practices that result from its grasping power. Military defeat, greed, and taxation ensure the transfer of goods from the provinces to Rome. Gold and silver, for instance, were procured from Spain where the mines had become state property, often through confiscations. Citrus wood grew along the North African coast and was greatly depleted by the end of the first century. The huge demand for and widespread use of ivory had a similar destructive impact on elephants in North Africa. Cinnamon, like other spices and pearls, probably derived from outside Rome's empire in the Far East (India, China). Romans, however, thought it originated with southern Arabian merchants who, it seems, deceived Roman merchants so as to protect their supplies from grasping Roman hands. Wheat and wine were frequently procured by taxes and tributes paid by provinces in kind. And the final reference to slaves disguises both the practice of coerced labor and the huge trade in human misery involving those taken as prisoners in war (70,000 from the Jewish war of 66–70, according to Josephus, *JW* 6.420), children and adults sold into slavery, exposed infants, and voluntary enslavements. The list represents losses from provinces and often the labor of numerous provincials who received minimal compensation.

The merchants continue their self-centered lament (18:14-17*a*). Without lamenting the city itself, they now lament the loss of such great wealth. Their description of the city recalls the description of the whore in 17:4, and rehearses items from the list of traded goods in 18:12-13. Economic exploitation defines Rome.

The third group of lamenters comprises those who travel the sea—shipmasters, seafarers, sailors, and traders (18:17*b*-19). They benefited from and effected the massive movement of goods to Rome. The destruction of "the great city" is a serious blow for their interests since they too "grew rich by her wealth" (18:19). Like the merchants, they note Rome's rapid demise "in one hour."

The judgment is total. In contrast to the list of Rome's exploitative trade (18:12-13), the angel catalogs its destruction (18:21-23). All sounds and activities end. There is no more music, artisan activity, food production, or light, human interaction. The chapter's audience is invited to rejoice "for God has given judgment for you against her" (18:20). This rejoicing contrasts the mourning and weeping of the kings (18:9), the merchants (18:11), and the mariners (18:19).

How does this judgment scene function for the seven churches of the cities in Asia addressed by Revelation (chaps. 2–3)? Why include the laments of the merchants and mariners? Will the audience mourn or rejoice? The chapter's address to the churches is clearly stated. A voice from heaven instructs them, "Come out of her, my people, so that you do not take part in her sins, and so that you do not share in her plagues" (18:4). The heavenly voice calls them to distance themselves from their culture and its economic practices. This emphasis is similar to that of the letters in chapters 2 and 3.

It is likely that among the churches in Asia were people involved in trade and transportation. Perhaps some in the church at Laodicea, for example, had accumulated significant wealth while others (as in the church of Smyrna) relied on work related to trade and transportation for daily survival. They saw no problem with this activity. It was necessary for their survival. The writer of Revelation disagrees. The angel and heavenly voice reveal the exploitative nature of Rome's economic activity and announce God's judgment on it. It is not just a matter of trade and artisan groups paying homage to the emperor in their gatherings. Their very participation in the imperial economy compromises them. The writer thinks their negotiation of Rome's economy is too accommodated. He presents them with a stark challenge in chapter 18 that requires them to change their way of living regardless of the cost. The chapter calls them to turn away from their cultural accommodation. It requires them to disengage from benefiting from the empire. They are to distance themselves from its activity. He does not, however, spell out his alternative. His emphasis falls on consequences. If they don't heed his call to "come out," they too will be caught up in the judgment. This is a costly challenge for some in the churches. For the writer of Revelation it is a life-and-death matter. We do not know if members of the seven churches complied with the writer's command.

Food

The New Testament writings engaged another everyday matter that involved negotiation of the empire, namely food. One scholar has shown that every chapter of Luke's Gospel contains references to food. The three synoptic Gospels (Mark, Matthew, Luke) feature Jesus' meals, including his last supper. Two of the seven "signs" that Jesus performs in John's Gospel involve providing wine (John 2:1-12) and feeding a crowd with bread and fish (6:1-14). Paul and Peter have a major confrontation and falling out over eating companions (Gal. 2:11-14). Paul rebukes the believers in Corinth for their divisive and humiliating meals (1 Cor. 11:17-34). James 3:15 and 1 John 3:16 urge providing for the hungry and needy. Rome's all-consuming trade that siphons off products from the provinces includes food (Rev. 18:13-14).

It is important to understand this concern with food within the context of the Roman imperial system. Food was about power.

Its production (based in land), distribution, and consumption reflected elite control. Accordingly, the wealthy and powerful enjoyed an abundant and diverse food supply. Quality and plentiful food was a marker of status and wealth, another indicator (like clothing, housing, transport, nonmanual labor, education, and so forth) that divided elites from nonelites. It established the former as privileged and powerful and the latter as inferior and of low entitlement. The latter struggled to acquire enough food as well as food of adequate nutritional value. For most, this was a constant struggle. And it was cyclic whereby most dropped below subsistence levels at times throughout each year. Food, then, displayed the injustice of the empire on a daily basis. The irony of this situation was that Roman propaganda claimed that one of the gifts of the Roman Empire to its inhabitants was fertility and abundance!

It is difficult for many of us in an age of well-stocked supermarkets, numerous restaurants, pervasive fast-food outlets, cookbooks, refrigerators, frozen and packaged food, obesity, faddish diets, and underreported starvation to understand problems with the food supply. The first-century world, though, was quite different. *Famines* were relatively rare because both elites and nonelites had strategies to prevent them. Elites provided handouts and controlled distribution; peasants diversified crops and stored any surplus. But whereas famines were rare, *food shortages* of varying intensities were frequent. They resulted from factors such as:

- nature: unfavorable weather, poor yields, crop disease, seasonal variations;
- agricultural practices: overcropping of land;
- the market: high prices, limited supply;
- political events: war, taxes, tribute, the priority of supplying Rome before other areas;
- distribution: attacks by pirates, poor storage, speculation by traders, self-interested elite control of storage;
- location: cities with surrounding areas unable to sustain a large urban population, distance from suppliers, distance from ports.

Our sources, mostly from elite authors, pay little attention to everyday struggles to procure food. They do, though, note times of special struggle—some local, some more regional—that were probably serious enough to threaten elites. The actual suffering for nonelites was of course much greater. The decades of the 40s and 50s CE—the time of Paul's mission—seem especially difficult. Early in the 40s the emperor Claudius authorized significant expansion of Rome's port Ostia after a shortage of grain. Flooding of the Nile in Egypt in the mid-40s caused damage to grain crops that seriously disrupted supply to Rome. Syria, Judea, and Jerusalem experienced severe food shortages around 46–48, probably the "worldwide" famine prophesied by Agabus in Acts 11:27-30.

The second half of the 40s and early 50s also saw flooding and crop loss in Greece. Evidence from Corinth attests that during the 40s and 50s an elite figure named Tiberius Claudius Dinippus was appointed three times as *curator annonae*. This costly office involved managing the limited grain supply in a time of crisis. The appointed person functioned as a benefactor. He used his own resources (and his influence to persuade other elite figures to do likewise) to purchase expensive grain supplies for the city. Dinippus's threefold appointment and honoring in inscriptions attest repeated shortages, Dinippus's considerable wealth, and a task satisfactorily undertaken. Some interpreters have seen Paul's reference to "the impending crisis" in 1 Corinthians 7:26 as a possible reference to a food shortage.

When elite authors do refer to food shortages, their central concern is usually not human suffering. Their primary concern is often the civic disturbances that inevitably accompany food shortages. Frequently the object of the urban crowds' desperation was elite officials, landowners, and their property. They were typically suspected, and not without some reason, of hoarding supplies, depriving nonelites of food, and driving up prices. Elites realized that such civic disorder, likely plunder, and personal injury threatened the hierarchical status quo over which they presided and from which they benefited. Practical responses varied. Occasionally price ceilings were fixed. Elites sponsored handouts. Cities appointed an official to oversee the crisis. Rarely, though, did cities establish emergency supplies.

Matthew

New Testament texts reflect and negotiate these realities in various ways. Probably addressed to followers in Antioch in Syria,

Matthew's Gospel, for example, mentions various aspects of the production of food: large landed estates, vineyards, slaves (20:1-16; 21:33-43), fishing (4:18-22), and manual labor (11:28-30). It names basic food items (bread, fish, wine, grain). It recognizes that food divides the powerful and the powerless. The ruler Herod Antipas, Rome's ally, enjoys a sumptuous birthday party (14:1-12) while others worry about what they will eat and drink (6:25-34). Some beg (20:29-34). There are food shortages (24:7).

Jesus attacks the Rome-allied, Jerusalem-based leadership for its control of the food supply. In describing the "harassed and helpless" nonelite as "sheep without a shepherd," he employs an image commonly used for rulers (9:36). The image especially recalls God's condemnation of the leaders in Ezekiel 34 for ruling the people with "force and harshness" (Ezek. 34:4). The rulers eat plentifully (34:2-3, 8) while they devour the sheep through harmful policies and practices (34:10). Ezekiel envisages their replacement with an agent of God's rule that will supply abundant food (34:13-31).

Matthew applies this critique to Rome's imperial system. In Matthew 12:1-8 Jesus opposes the ruling group's attempt to forbid gathering food on the Sabbath. In 15:5-6 he rejects their efforts of encouraging gifts to the temple that deprive the vulnerable elderly of resources needed for food. In 23:23-24 their focus on tithing "mint, dill, and cumin" looks ridiculous compared to their neglect of weightier matters such as justice, faithfulness, and mercy. Attention to these last three matters would see a radical reform of the empire and of the food supply. But of course elite guardians of the empire are not interested in reform. For his challenges, Jesus dies.

How are followers of Jesus to negotiate this world? Instead of imitating urban culture and appealing to wealthy civic benefactors, the Gospel places responsibility with each disciple (compare the similar response to the famine in Acts 11:29, and Paul's collection in 1 Cor. 16:1-4). Disciples are to share whatever food they have with those who are hungry. One of the traditional "acts of mercy" required of disciples (almsgiving, 6:2-4) comprises providing food (Prov. 25:21; Tob. 1:16-17). Food is shared not to enhance one's honor and reputation, but for the good of the other. Disciples are also to fast (6:16-18). Fasting usually means forgoing food. However, the prophet Isaiah describes "true fasting" as countering injustice, freeing the oppressed, feeding the hungry, and providing hospitality to the homeless and naked (Isa. 58:6-10). Supplying food to the hungry, the "least of these," is a criterion for judgment (25:35, 37, 42, 44). Such work, required of all disciples regardless of levels of resources, constitutes those who are blessed as hungering and thirsting for justice (5:6). It contributes to alternative social and economic interactions. The instruction to pray, "Give us this day our daily bread," sustains such work and frames it in the context of prayer for the coming of God's empire and the doing of God's will "on earth as it is in heaven" (6:9-13). Supplying food is God's will.

In addition to these strategies, the Gospel includes two scenes in which Jesus enacts God's purposes for fertility and abundant food. Twice Jesus feeds large crowds (14:13-21; 15:32-39). He takes a limited human supply (a desert; large numbers; few resources) and produces so much food that all are fed and there are leftovers. These scenes enact visions from prophetic traditions that depict God's future reign and the completion of God's purposes as a feast of abundant, good-quality food. Isaiah envisions a feast on Mount Zion (the mountain in Matt. 15:29) "of rich food, a feast of well-aged wines, of rich food filled with marrow" (Isa. 25:6-10; Ezek. 34:25-31) "for all peoples." Apocalyptic writers contemporary with Matthew such as 4 Ezra 7–8, 2 Baruch 72–73, and Apocalypse of Abraham 21 similarly envisage the completion of God's purposes in establishing a world of abundant fertility. Such visions of God's future work, like Matthew's, show Rome's propaganda claims that it had already created a world of abundance and plenty to be false and presumptuous. God's justice-bringing work will reverse the inadequate food supply that marks Rome's empire.

The establishment of God's reign in a new heaven and earth (Matt. 19:28; 24:35) will also restore access to land, necessary for food supply. Recalling the situation of Psalm 37, Jesus promises the suffering poor ("the meek") that God will overcome the oppressive powerful and rich. God will reverse the current injustice and the poor will inherit the land (Matt. 5:5 evoking Ps. 37). God's final victory will establish God's justice and replace malnutrition and inadequate food with abundant food. Disciples anticipate this future "meal of all meals" in the meantime by eating together in honor of Jesus "until that day" (26:26-29; cf. 8:11-12).

Meals and Table Fellowship

Food—either its abundance or its lack—represents the power structures of the Roman Empire. Likewise, meals depict the empire's patterns of social interactions. Meals were occasions of social bonding, solidarity, intimacy, and unity. Guest lists indicated inclusion or exclusion from a group, thereby reinforcing group or class boundaries. But elite meals also enhanced social obligations among guests as equals or inferiors. They required a reciprocal act. Meals underlined social stratification. Guests were seated according to their perceived social standing. They were served different quantities and qualities of food on different quality tableware.

Luke's Gospel presents Jesus performing his ministry at meals. He does so at meals not only by teaching (as a distinguished teacher in the Greco-Roman banquet-symposium tradition), but also by acting out his message. Particularly prominent in Luke's accounts are Jesus' eating companions and the controversy they cause.

In Luke 5:27-32, Jesus eats with Levi and other tax collectors. Pharisees and scribes, people of power and privilege, protest. Tax collectors contracted with ruling elites—Romans, local landowners, city rulers—to collect tolls, customs, and duties. They collected enough to pay the contracted amount and to pocket the profit. They were widely despised as extortionists and thieves. In this scene, the elite observers call them sinners. In their view, Jesus should not associate with such people whom they regard as unfaithful to God and beyond God's purposes. Jesus does not accept those boundaries. His mission is to bring the good news of God's favor to all people, especially to those regarded by elite circles as marginal and unworthy (4:18-19). Jesus acts out his inclusive, loving message and mission by eating with them.

In response, the elite (7:30) attack Jesus' reputation by calling him "a glutton and a drunkard, a friend of tax collectors and sinners" (7:34). The language of "glutton and drunkard" is used in Deuteronomy 21:18-21 to identify a rebellious son who is expelled (by stoning) from a community. The elite have decided Jesus has broken too many boundaries and is too deviant to be acceptable. He immediately confirms their suspicions—and enacts his mission—by accepting the loving actions of a "sinful" woman at a meal in a Pharisee's house. He extends God's inclusive forgiveness to her (7:36-50).

Chapter 14 builds a collage of meal scenes to depict God's transforming empire or reign manifested in Jesus' ministry. In 14:1-6, at a meal at a Pharisee's house on a Sabbath, Jesus extends God's merciful power to a sick man and heals him. In 14:7-11, Jesus attacks the elite's social honor code by criticizing the practice of seating people according to their social status. His attack rejects a foundation of imperial society, namely social stratification and hierarchy. In 14:12-14, he attacks the practice of reciprocity. This practice formed part of the patronage system, which understood "gifts" or favors or invitations to obligate people to reciprocate in equal and appropriate ways. The practice reinforced divisions between elites and nonelites because nonelites lacked resources to reciprocate equally. Instead they were obligated to provide services and goods. Jesus proposes a different pattern of social interaction, one that rejects insider-outsider/privileged-powerless boundaries. Instead it values generosity and inclusion, especially of the socially despised (14:13). In this way, social interaction embodies and imitates God's purposes. In 14:15-24, Jesus reinforces the point by telling the parable of the "great dinner." The host includes nonelites and the destitute who cannot reciprocate and whose presence constitutes a different social interaction.

In these meal scenes, Jesus counters basic social patterns of imperial society that were encapsulated in meal etiquette: valuing social status, stratification, hierarchy; reciprocity; elite/nonelite boundaries; and exclusion. He verbalizes and enacts alternative societal patterns of inclusion and disregard for social status. He attests the inclusive hospitality that Luke's audience is to practice in continuing his mission.

Sickness and Healing

Beyond controlling access to food and shaping patterns of social interaction expressed in meals, the imperial food system had another disastrous consequence for most inhabitants of the empire. It made them sick.

The "Mediterranean diet" is theoretically healthful. Staples such

115

as cereals, olives, wine, and legumes supply energy, protein, vitamins B and E, calcium, and iron. However, numerous factors such as limited quantities of food, inferior quality, and uneven supplies reduced its *actual* healthfulness, resulting in widespread malnutrition. Malnutrition was evident in diseases of deficiency and of infection. Deficiency diseases included painful bladder stones from lack of animal products, eye diseases from vitamin A deficiency and diets low in animal-derived products and green vegetables, and rickets or limb deformity from vitamin D deficiency.

Malnutrition also renders people more vulnerable to infectious diseases such as malaria, diarrhea, and dysentery. High population densities in cities; poverty; inadequate sewage and garbage disposal; limited sanitation; inadequate water supply distribution and unhygienic storage in cisterns; transmission of diseases in public baths; the presence of animals and feces; flies, mosquitoes, and other insects; and ineffective medical intervention ensured widespread infection. Swollen eyes, skin rashes, and lost limbs were common, as were cholera, typhus, and the plague bacillus. Meningitis, measles, mumps, scarlet fever, and smallpox affected many, causing deafness and blindness.

Not surprisingly, mortality rates were high and age spans short. Up to 50 percent of children died by age ten. Child-raising practices such as denying protein-rich, infection-fighting colostrum to newborns and early weaning onto nutritionally inadequate foods contributed to high infant mortality rates. Swaddling contributed to limb deformation. Estimates of age spans suggest that while elites could live into their sixties or seventies, the life span of nonelites was much shorter, often around thirty.

The Gospels depict the consequences of a world in which the food supply is precarious and its nutritional quality poor. The sick and physically damaged pervade the Gospels. John's Gospel features three stories in which Jesus brings healing to the official's son (John 4:46-54, fever), the crippled man (5:1-18), and the blind man (chap. 9). These healing stories attest to lengthy suffering and the poor quality of people's lives. The crippled man, for example, has been ill for thirty-eight years, has no caring support, and exists with many others who are blind, lame, and paralyzed (5:3-5). The blind man is a beggar (9:8) and seems distanced from his parents (9:19-23). Healing means not only restored health but a new life and social experience.

Matthew includes numerous summary passages referring to many diseases and healings (Matt. 4:23-25; 9:35; 11:4-5; 12:15-17; 14:34-36; 15:29-31; 21:14). He also personalizes the suffering and transformation, with individual healing scenes, either in sequences (chaps. 8–9; 12:9-14, 22), or alone (15:21-28; 17:14-20; 20:29-34). Among the specified diseases are contagious leprosy (8:1-4; 11:5), as well as blindness (9:27-31; 11:5; 12:22; 15:30-31; 20:30; 21:14), pains (4:24), and various deformities and paralysis (4:24; 8:6; 9:2; 11:5; 12:9-14; 15:30; 21:14).

Also to be noted are studies that link imperial and oppressive contexts with psychosomatic illness and demonic possession. Scholars have observed the prevalence of physical symptoms of pains, menstrual disorders, muteness, muscular rigidity, and paralysis in contexts of exploitation and trauma. In Matthew's Gospel a centurion has a paralyzed slave (8:6; son?), and there are other paralyzed folk (4:24; 9:2, 6), along with the hemorrhaging woman (9:20-22), the shriveled up (12:10), and the mute/deaf (9:32-33; 11:5; 12:22; 15:30-31). Matthew also refers to numerous demoniacs (4:24; 8:16, 28, 33; 9:32; 12:22; 15:22).

Jesus' healings and exorcisms are direct confrontations with the effects of Roman rule. In his exorcisms he engages the demonic power "behind the throne" (4:8) and overcomes it (8:26-34). In giving new life to demoniacs and the sick, Jesus rolls back the destructive impact of the empire. He asserts God's life-giving purposes (Matt. 11:2-6; 12:15-21), and manifests God's empire or reign (12:28). In so doing he anticipates the final establishment of God's purposes that will be marked not only by abundance and fertility (see page 113), but also by physical wholeness. Healing accompanies the feedings (14:14; 15:29-31). The prophet Isaiah envisions the establishment of God's reign as a time that reverses the physical damage to persons caused by empires. "The eyes of the blind shall be opened, and the ears of the deaf unstopped; then the lame shall leap like a deer, and the tongue of the speechless sing for joy" (Isa. 35:5-6). Matthew quotes this passage in 11:2-6 to interpret Jesus' healings as signifying the presence of God's empire in the midst of Rome's and anticipating its future establishment.

Followers of Jesus continue this healing work that signifies the presence of God's empire and anticipates its future establishment. Paul reminds the Corinthians that he worked "signs and wonders

117

and mighty works" among them (2 Cor. 12:12). Acts narrates healings performed by Peter and John (Acts 3:1-10), the apostles (5:12),
Philip (8:6-8), Paul and Barnabas (14:3), and Paul (19:11-12).
Matthew's Jesus commands disciples, "Cure the sick, raise the
dead, cleanse the lepers, cast out demons" (Matt. 10:8). James
exhorts the sick to call the elders for anointing with oil and prayer
(James 5:14-15).

Revelation places this healing activity in the context of the completion of God's purposes. In the new Jerusalem that replaces condemned Babylon/Rome, there will be no more death, mourning,
crying, and pain (Rev. 21:4). God will completely reverse the sick-
ening impact of Rome's empire, replacing sickness and disease
with new life, abundance, and wholeness.

Conclusion

Wealth or its lack, food or its lack, and health or its lack comprise three everyday expressions of the Roman imperial system. In
this chapter I have observed a number of ways in which some
New Testament writers negotiated these everyday realities.

CHAPTER 8

Further Dynamics of Resistance

T he hierarchical social interactions and exploitative structures of the Roman Empire fostered social resentment, anger, and hostility. There were no democratic processes of reform. Instead, New Testament writers offer, as we have seen, various ways of negotiating Rome's empire. We have analyzed this diverse negotiation as it involves

- the empire's hierarchical structure (chapter 1);
- different evaluations of the empire (chapter 2);
- ruling faces of the empire (chapter 3);
- places of the empire, including city, countryside, and temples (chapters 4-5);
- imperial theology (chapter 6);
- economics, food, and sickness and healing (chapter 7).

This concluding chapter looks further at some dynamics involved in resisting Rome's rule. We have observed that often accommodation and resistance coexist. But resistance takes different forms. It can be violent and nonviolent, hidden and open, directly confrontational or more concerned with the distinctive practices and theology of an alternative community. In this chapter I will discuss three expressions of resistance: imagining Rome's

119

violent overthrow, employing disguised and ambiguous protest, and using flattery.

1. Imagining Rome's Violent Overthrow

As I noted in chapter 1, we often think of public, violent protest as the obvious antithesis to domination and the only or main form of resistance. Violent revolts against Rome did occur in the first century, for example, in Germany, Gaul, Britain, and Judea. Bandit groups and popular rebel figures who attacked elite property and personnel emerged, especially in rural areas. Violence also broke out in cities. In both Jerusalem and Antioch in Syria, for example, crowds around 70 CE attacked and burned the debt records building.

The New Testament writers forbid followers of Jesus from making physically violent attacks against Roman targets, as we have seen (Matt. 26:52-53). Jesus names violence as the defining feature of Rome's empire, but is to be absent from his followers committed to God's empire (John 18:36).

In a sense, the New Testament writers can insist on Christians not using violence against Rome because it is God's task to destroy Rome's empire. Christians do not need to oppose Rome violently in the present because God will soon violently overthrow the empire. Oppressed peoples often entertain visions of the violent destruction of their oppressors. New Testament writers imagine God punishing and destroying Rome's empire just as God has confounded Egyptian pharaohs, Assyrian rulers, and the Babylonian Empire in the past. This overthrow will be very public and cosmic. New Testament writings offer various scenarios of this overthrow.

Punitive Rhetoric

One scenario directs punitive rhetoric against elites, promising their destruction and the reversal of the social order. Paul repeatedly declares the end of Rome's ruling authorities. In 1 Corinthians 15:24 he proclaims that Christ will "destroy every ruler and every authority and power" when God's empire is established.

Paul's statements are "in-house" and hidden in that they are directed to believers and are not for a public audience. The Gospels also present Jesus speaking publicly to and about elites. Jesus utters words of indignation against them, negating and countering their values and self-benefiting societal structures. Luke's Jesus, for example, denounces in a series of woes or prophetic judgments those who are rich and full, promising that God will reverse the status quo (Luke 6:24-25). Subsequently, he condemns the Jerusalem rulers with a series of woes in 11:37-54 directed against their "greed and wickedness" (11:39). They will not enter God's reign (13:28-29), and their center of power, Jerusalem, will be destroyed (19:41-44).

Mark's Jesus identifies Rome and the military power of its legions as demonic (Mark 5:1-20). He anticipates God's powerful destruction of Rome by casting the demons called Legion into the sea (5:9-13). In Mark 7:1-13, he condemns the temple-based Jerusalem leaders for "abandon[ing] the commandment of God" (7:8) and "making void the word of God" (7:13). He tells peasants in Galilean villages not to support the temple because offerings to God that deprived the vulnerable elderly of support violated the command to honor parents. Jesus' condemnation of the leaders means their inevitable punishment. In 8:15 he warns people to beware of the leaders as "yeast," a reference to their corrupting evil that results from their rejection of God's purposes. In all the Gospels, Jesus' attack on the temple (see the discussion in chapter 5, above) is an open and public confrontation with the leaders. He punctures the societal order by enacting its judgment for failing to enact God's purposes. For this open and direct challenge, he dies.

John the Baptist also directly confronts and verbally condemns the Jerusalem leadership, telling them that "even now the ax is lying at the root of the trees" (Matt. 3:7-10). Prophets used the ax image to denote God's judgment on and destruction of the Assyrian (Isa. 10:33-34; Ezek. 31) and Babylonian Empires (Dan. 4:9-27). But the ax was also a symbol of Roman authority. It was part of the *fasces*, a bundle of rods and ax paraded by Roman rulers as an intimidating symbol of Rome's power to ensure submission by beating and decapitating. John the Baptist turns the image back on Rome's provincial allies as a symbol of God's order that will destroy Rome and its allies. He adds a further image of judgment by declaring that not only will the trees be cut down, they will be burned. Rome had burned Jerusalem in 70 CE by destroying the city. John's promise is that God will destroy Rome. Herod, Rome's puppet, ensures John dies—by beheading him (Matt. 14:8-12).

Imagined Destruction

Other scenarios imagine the violent judgment that follows from Jesus' return, and precedes the transformation of the world through the full establishment of God's empire. Those who are "ashamed" of Jesus and his words now will be condemned at his return (Mark 8:38). Those who deny Jesus now will be denied (condemned) by him then (Luke 12:8).

Matthew envisions Rome's overthrow in 24:27-31 at the return of Jesus. The first part of Matthew 24 emphasizes that discipleship in the time before Jesus' return is marked by increasing turmoil and requires faithful endurance and mission (24:12-13). But when it happens, Jesus' "coming" will be spectacular like flashes of lightning (24:27). Lightning often denotes God's power and presence (Exod. 19:16). But it is also associated with Jupiter and signals either the favor or disfavor of the gods for Rome expressed in earthly events such as battles and accession to power. This ambivalent reference to lightning indicates that Jesus' return means a clash of powers. God's sovereignty collides with Rome's.

Jesus' return is called a "coming" (Matt. 24:3, 27). The Greek noun *parousia* similarly indicates a collision of powers. It denotes God's powerful presence as well as the approach of a Roman emperor, general, or governor to a city where he is received with honor and deference. Jesus is named in 24:27 as the "Son of Man." This description evokes the figure in Daniel 7 who acts on God's behalf, destroys all human empires, and establishes God's "everlasting dominion" (Dan. 7:14).

Verse 28 describes the destruction from Jesus' coming as Son of Man. "Wherever the corpse is, there the eagles will be gathered" (literal translation). Eagles (not the mistaken translation, "vultures") represent imperial powers subject to God's purposes (Deut. 28:49). The eagle was of course the symbol of the Roman Empire. Soldiers carried eagle images into battle. In verse 28, the eagles, symbols of Roman military power, are gathered with corpses. Both the eagle images and soldiers are destroyed in the final battle against Jesus' forces. Other Jewish texts from around Matthew's time depict a final battle between God's forces and Rome, with Rome being destroyed (4 Ezra 11–13; 2 Baruch 39–40; Qumran's War Scroll).

God's victory is accompanied in verse 29 by cosmic signs. The sun darkens, as does the moon, and stars fall from heaven. Some understood these "powers of heaven" as solar, lunar, and astral deities that blessed and guided Rome. God's victory at Jesus' coming extinguishes these cosmic deities in judgment and reasserts God's sovereignty over this part of God's creation (Gen. 1). Jesus' coming is "lights-out" time for Rome.

A sign or military emblem appears in the heavens announcing God's victory and the establishment of God's empire or reign (24:30). Jesus sends out angels, who with a trumpet call—a conventional call to battle—gather God's people. God's empire destroys Rome and establishes God's purposes.

There is an interesting paradox in this scene of imagined destruction. It presents Rome's downfall as very public and cosmic. But the vision is covert and hidden. It is not public knowledge or made known to Rome. Only those who are committed to Jesus and hear the "in-house" gospel know it. The vision functions not to warn Rome, but to assure Jesus' followers of justice and transformation at God's violent and cosmic intervention. It sustains them in living out faithfully their alternative community and understanding of life.

It is not surprising that the New Testament writings envision Rome's violent punishment, reversal of societal order, and powerful overthrow. These writings are influenced by the cultural circumstances of military violence and subjugation in which they originate. The values and practices of those who dominate shape the oppressed. Oppressed peoples absorb the cultural ethos, which constantly models violent power as the means to a very desirable end. Accordingly, they want to be in charge. They want what they hate. As we saw in chapters 1 and 2, numerous studies have shown that in their "hidden transcripts" oppressed people often imagine violent revenge on their oppressors and a reversal of roles. They become like that which they oppose. They envision themselves exercising power and enjoying wealth and status. That is, their fantasies of reversal and revenge often imitate their oppressors both in means—the use of violent and overwhelming power—and in outcome—the gaining of wealth, power, and status. This tension reflects their hybrid existence, caught up in the intersection between the culture of the oppressed and their own culture as the oppressed.

Imaginary Violence and Revelation

The book of Revelation graphically imagines Rome's violent defeat. Throughout, it anticipates, describes, and celebrates the downfall of demonic Rome, destroyed in judgment by God. Chapter 18 envisions its economic and political collapse, as we saw in chapter 7, above. Chapter 19:17-21 pictures a final battle in which Rome's military might—the backbone of the empire and the means of enforcing its will and deterring revolt—is defeated by the army of the returned Christ. Violence is even threatened in chapter 2 against those in the church at Thyatira who disagree with the writer. The Son of God threatens to throw a leader called Jezebel "on a bed," bring great distress to her followers, and kill her children/followers (2:21-23a) if they persist in their accommodationist way of life. These scenarios of violent judgment and downfall are clearly presented from the outset as a vision (1:10-20; 9:17; 18:1). They comprise a sustained fantasy of violent revenge.

But Revelation is more complex than violent revenge to reverse the fortunes of the downtrodden, or a vision of God violently accomplishing what humans cannot imagine doing for themselves. The book's violence reflects the interaction of various traditions comprising not only the dynamic of the oppressor and the oppressed, but also traditions from the Hebrew Bible about God's ways, as well as New Testament traditions about Jesus. That means, among other things, that the visions of violent punishment are qualified in various ways. Much more is happening than God's unmitigated revenge. These seven qualifications do not excuse the violence, but they do place it in a much broader context and show how complicated is its role.

The desire for God to punish Rome, for example, is qualified by a recognition that empire brings about its own demise. In 5:6 the Lamb takes the scroll and starts to open its seals. As each seal is broken, a terrible consequence occurs for the world. The first four

124

seals, described in 6:1-8, release conquest, war, economic exploitation, famine, and pestilence. In one sense these disasters depict
God's violent punishment. Yet the violent destruction does not
come about because God intervenes. Conquest, war, economic
exploitation, and famine are expressions and consequences of
empire. Military power was foundational for Rome's empire.
Economic exploitation was the elite's mode of life. Famine and
disease were inevitable consequences (see chapter 7, above). These
are everyday imperial realities well known to the empire's inhabitants. They are presented as God's judgment. God's judgment,
already taking place, is less about angry thunderbolts than it is
about a permissive stance toward the world. God allows Rome to
experience the consequences of its own rule. It seems justice,
rather than revenge, is operative.

Yet revenge is not far away because God's permissive justice
means injustice for many. There is tragic fallout from God's nonac-
tion or permissive stance. Not only is there general suffering, the
fifth seal reveals martyrs killed by empire (6:9-11). They cry out to
God, "How long will it be before you judge and avenge our
blood?" The sixth seal reveals a cosmic catastrophe as the world
falls apart (6:12-17). This is the "wrath of the Lamb" at work
(6:16-17).

A second factor qualifies the desire for revenge. In chapters 8
and 9, seven trumpets blow in sequence. As each of the first four
trumpets blows, terrible disasters happen on earth and throughout the cosmos (8:6-12). These disasters echo the ten plagues that
afflicted Pharaoh before he let the enslaved Israelites depart from
Egypt (Exod. 7–12). A third of the earth is destroyed, along with a
mountain and a third of the rivers, and a third of the sun, moon,
and stars. The fifth trumpet releases a hoard of locusts or scorpi-
onlike creatures from the underworld that attack people opposed
to God (9:1-11). The sixth trumpet produces an attack that kills a
third of the population. As with the first four seals, this attack is
a consequence of empire. Empires always elicit challengers.
The attackers resemble Rome's archrival, the Parthian Empire
(9:13-19).

What is significant about this sequence of trumpet-released disasters is its limited extent and purpose. The disasters destroy not
everything, but a third of the targets. Mercy tempers the destruction.

Verses 20 and 21 make very clear that this violence is to be understood not as revenge or judgment but as a merciful warning. It is intended to bring about repentance. So the first trumpet destroys not the whole earth, but only (!) a third (8:7). The locusts/scorpions are allowed to torture but not kill (9:5). They can target only those opposed to God's purposes (9:4). The desire for violent punishment is modified by a merciful chance for repentance. However, verses 20 and 21 recognize that the attempt fails.

There is a third qualification to the desire for violent revenge that involves God's use of life-giving power. The central figure in God's purposes is "a Lamb standing as if it had been slaughtered" (5:6). In the previous verse, one of the elders invites the seer, "See, the Lion of the tribe of Judah, the Root of David" (5:5). But in an amazing juxtaposition, what he is invited to see differs greatly from what he actually sees. In 5:6, the powerful conquering Lion, king of the beasts, turns out to be a "Lamb standing." Rather than causing suffering by exerting great power, the Lamb appears to have suffered at the hands of power. Instead of slaughtering, it has been slaughtered, a verb that commonly represents imperial violence in Revelation (6:4, 9). The agent of God's purposes has been a victim of imperial violence (crucifixion) but he has not been destroyed. He stands, a reference to Jesus' resurrection, and is in the heavens (his ascension or vindication by God). God has outpowered and triumphed over Rome, but has done so not with an act of violence but with a powerful act of giving life to one who was broken and killed. God's way of working is an alternative to Rome's methods.

But, fourth, if the Lamb manifests God's life-giving purpose, what about the battle scene in 19:17-21? Again the violent fantasy is qualified, here by the choice of weapons. The Lamb, or in chapter 19 the rider on the white horse (19:11-21), fights not with literal weapons but with a sword that comes from his mouth (19:15). He wears a robe stained not with the blood of others but with his own blood given for others (19:13). He is identified as the "Word of God" (19:13) who reveals or communicates God's purposes. He captures the beast and his prophet (19:20) and kills the rest with his sword, but it is "the sword that came from his mouth" (19:21). God does not imitate imperial military violence to achieve victory but accomplishes it through revealing, persuading, and judging words.

A fifth qualification of the fantasy of violent revenge emerges in another cycle of judgments in chapters 15 and 16. After sequences of opened seals (chap. 6, consequences of empire) and blown trumpets (chaps. 8–9, warnings to urge repentance), this third sequence in chapters 15 and 16 expresses God's judgment through seven bowls or plagues (again echoing the Exodus plagues). These bowls or plagues express the "wrath of God" (16:1, 19) against those who "did not repent of their [evil] deeds" (16:9, 11), a reference back to the trumpets of chapters 8 and 9 and 9:20-21 in particular. There is a final battle (16:12-16) and great destruction only after people have been given the chance to repent. An angel declares God's "judgments are true and just," and celebrates the revenge: "It is what they deserve!" (16:5-7).

Yet, sixth, juxtaposed to this violence and destruction is another thread, one of salvation, transformation, and inclusion. The two chapters begin with a hymn of praise (15:3-4). The hymn does not gloat over enemies destroyed. It does not mock the vanquished. Rather, it praises God for being "just and true" and "king of the nations." And instead of celebrating judgment and destruction, it declares, "All nations will come and worship before you" (15:4). The overarching agenda seems to be salvation, not vengeful destruction.

A similar emphasis occurs at the end of the book in 21:24-26. Even though the nations are supposedly destroyed (19:15), they come to live by the light (saving presence) of God that shines from the new Jerusalem. The "kings of the earth" are destroyed in 19:19-21 as God's opponents, yet they are drawn to this light and to the city's ever open gates (21:24-25). Revelation's vision ends with healing for the nations (22:2). A vision of transformation and inclusion for all people affected through God's life-giving power completes the book.

We should also note as a seventh qualification that Revelation insists that humans do not use violence to attack the empire. Followers of the "Lamb standing as if it had been slaughtered" (5:6), who live in the seven churches of the province of Asia where economic, civic, and religious participation in the empire was woven into the fabric of everyday life, are to employ the same means of resistance as the Lamb. They negotiate Rome's world by bearing "faithful witness" (1:5), refusing to compromise, and by coming "out from her" (18:4). Their faithfulness means social and economic hardship, even suffering martyrdom, as the consequence of their nonviolent faithfulness, if necessary. These faithful witnesses comprise the army of God and the Lamb (chap. 7). They gain victory not by violence, not by causing suffering to others, but by faithfulness (7:14-17). Their martyrdom results from active but nonviolent resistance that refuses to be intimidated by the empire's violence and denies it the power to determine their loyalties.

Such imaginings of violent and cosmic overthrow, reversal, and punishment of Rome sustained, and were sustained among, powerless groups of followers of Jesus. Committed to God's purposes manifested in Jesus, these groups envision the day when their alternative practices and social interactions replace Rome's oppressive system through God's intervention. These imaginings are the in-group protests of an alternative community, directed against Rome but not made public or expressed openly to Rome. They speak "truth about power" rather than "truth to power." They do, though, undergird practices of direct and open (nonviolent) confrontation with imperial officials and with neighbors and fellow guild or artisan group members, such as not sacrificing to the emperor and costly withdrawal from economic and social participation in the empire.

2. Disguised and Ambiguous Protest

As we saw in chapters 1 and 2, dominated groups commonly feign compliance in order to survive while engaging in disguised acts of resistance that express their refusal to accept the elite's agenda. These protests are carefully calculated, self-protective, self-dignifying, and often ambiguous. They are often directed as much internally as toward external enemies.

For example, the scene in which Jesus enters Jerusalem on Palm Sunday is full of ambiguity and disguise (Mark 11:1-10; Matt. 21:1-11). The setting is Passover, but Jesus employs symbols that, for those in the know, point to God's future intervention.

Rome allowed the Passover festival to take place. Even though it could threaten Roman control because it celebrated the people's freedom from slavery to the Egyptians, Rome sought to control this desire by allowing limited expression. Jesus acts within what is sanctioned. Everything seems to be under control.

Jesus enters Jerusalem from the Mount of Olives. This might appear to be an ordinary everyday place, but for those in the know it has great significance. It is the place from which God will exercise the final judgment and salvation, according to Zechariah 14. Jesus evokes dangerous traditions that the Jerusalem rulers do not emphasize and the Roman rulers probably do not know. He appeals to an alternative or "little" tradition over against more acceptable traditions that sanction the status quo (often called "Great Traditions"). He exploits the ambiguity of the ordinary and the special. He disguises his resisting message in this ambiguity.

A similar thing happens with the entry itself. There was a set protocol for Roman officials, such as emperors, generals, or governors, entering a city. It involved the elite escorting the official into the city, welcoming crowds, hymns, speeches of welcome, and offering sacrifice in the city temple. This protocol acknowledged and submitted to Roman greatness in terms of its power and ability to dominate.

Most of these elements appear in Jesus' entrance scene. Jesus processes. Welcoming crowds celebrate. They recite a hymn (Psalm 118). He goes into the temple, though, to announce judgment on its death-bringing impact. Absent is any welcome from the elites. Jesus is not recognized for his greatness and power to dominate. In fact, the scene is preceded by Jesus' declaration that he has come to serve not be served (20:28) and by a demonstration of his life-giving service in the healing of two blind men (20:29-34). His entry emphasizes a way of life and practices antithetical to Rome's.

Moreover, about half of the scene involves procuring the donkey. An entering general or emperor would ride a warhorse or chariot, not an everyday lowly beast of burden like a donkey. The donkey was a common symbol of Gentile derision and scorn toward Jews. Some Gentile writers claimed that Jews worshiped a donkey's head in the temple. Jesus identifies with the underdonkey. He appears to be a common poor peasant riding an everyday beast just as others probably did.

Yet the donkey was ambiguous. For those in the know, the donkey had a much greater significance. It is the animal that God is to ride into Jerusalem in Zechariah 9 when God defeats those who, like Rome, resist God's purposes, and that establishes God's reign in full. Mark leaves this significance of the donkey unstated and disguised, assuming his audience will know this inside information (Mark 11:7). Matthew spells it out. He inserts in Matthew 21:4-5 a quote from Zechariah 9:9, which refers to God's entry to Jerusalem, to make sure we understand the significance of Jesus' ambiguous and hidden action.

Similarly, ambiguity surrounds the psalm that the crowds recite. They shout (with slightly different wording in Mark and Matthew), "Hosanna to the son of David. Blessed is the one who comes in the name of the Lord." They recite from Psalm 118 to celebrate God's saving of the people by victory over the nations. It was an especially appropriate and common psalm for reciting at Passover in celebrating freedom from Egypt. But in relation to Jesus the psalm takes on new significance for those in the know. It does not just look back to the past. It joins with the references to Zechariah 9 through 14 concerning the "Mount of Olives" and the "donkey" to anticipate God's final salvation and victory over opposing forces such as Rome. The psalm has meaning hidden from the ruling powers but known to Jesus' followers. What appears to be a permitted festival celebration takes on hidden, subversive, threatening significance.

We can think of Jesus' entrance as a kind of street theater or acted parable. Jesus uses ambiguity to enact a message that restores dignity and offers hope to those suffering under Rome's rule. His actions are, for those in the know, extremely threatening to Rome, yet on the outside they appear to be nothing more than participation in the permitted festival activities. He exploits the festival occasion to both conceal and to reveal God's purposes, avoiding direct confrontation with the rulers while engaging in a hidden protest.

When he enters the temple in the next scene, though, he takes a very different approach. In overturning tables and citing prophets like Jeremiah, he openly and directly confronts the temple establishment with its vast economic, political, religious, and societal power (see chapter 5, above). He forcefully punctures the ruling order to expose its exploitation. For this attack, he dies.

Ambiguous Disguised Practices for Followers

Jesus' followers are to practice the same sort of ambiguity and indirect protest. Such actions will not change the system in which the powerless have no access to political power. But they restore dignity, anticipate another way of life, encourage initiative, and protest the injustice of the present. We will briefly look at two incidents.

Sermon on the Mount

In the Sermon on the Mount, Jesus instructs disciples (Matt. 5:39-41): "Do not [violently] resist an evildoer. But if anyone strikes you on the right cheek, turn the other also; and if anyone wants to sue you and take your coat, give your cloak as well; and if anyone forces you to go one mile, go also the second mile." These strange instructions have often been misunderstood as Jesus instructing his followers to be wimpy doormats who are passive before injustice. More accurately, these instructions provide examples of ambiguous, active, but nonviolent resistance.

Basic to them is the refusal to meet violence with violence. The NRSV translation, "Do not resist an evildoer," makes no sense since Jesus' instructions from 5:21-37 have exhorted disciples to resist doing evil! The verb used here indicates "armed resistance" or "violent struggle." The issue is not whether one should resist or not. It is not a choice between fight or flight, violence or passivity. The issue concerns *how* to resist. A better translation would read, "Do not violently resist an evildoer." Jesus outlaws violent revenge (5:38) but advocates active nonviolent resistance.

Jesus' first example engages social inequalities. He refers to the insulting slap in the face from a superior to an inferior—master to slave, rich to poor, Roman to provincial (cf. 26:67). The slap is intended to humiliate. Jesus urges a different, active, but nonviolent response. Instead of continuing the cycle of violence in retaliation or leaving it unchecked with passivity, the inferior chooses to show that he or she has not been humiliated or beaten into submission. Turning the other cheek refuses submission, asserts dignity, rejects humiliation, and challenges what is supposed to demean. To the superior, the gesture is ambiguous: Has submission been achieved or not?

Jesus' second example concerns a court proceeding over economic inequalities. It probably involves a poor person who has provided a coat or outer garment as a pledge for a loan he cannot now repay and is about to lose his land. Giving up his cloak or

inner garment means stripping himself naked in court. It symbolizes the stripping away of property and dignity. It exposes, among
other things, the basic humanity of the poor as well as the powerful person's heartless demand.

Jesus' third demand concerns Rome's military power. The
"force" involves Rome's right to requisition labor, transport, and
lodging from subject people (see Matt. 27:32). Jesus' instruction to
carry the soldier's pack an extra mile appears initially to be compliance. But like the previous two examples, it is an active strategy
for refusing to be humiliated by claiming initiative and asserting
one's dignity to the discomfort of the oppressor. Going the second
mile is a surprising action. It refuses to deal with Rome only in its
terms. It reconfigures the power arrangement. The oppressed has
decided the action, not the soldier. It places the soldier off guard
and out of control, wondering if the provincial is being helpful or
mischievous, and wondering if he will be reported for making the
provincial do two miles.

Jesus' fourth example (5:42) concerns not refusing those who
beg. The action focuses not on wealth but on doing justice. The
four examples provide imaginative, creative, active strategies for
unsettling the power arrangements, restoring dignity, and break-
ing the cycle of violence. They assert initiative, dignity,
and humanity in ambiguous ways over against injustice and
oppression.

Paying Taxes

Jesus gives another instruction about paying taxes that both
hides yet expresses resistance. In Matthew 17:24-27, Jesus instructs
Peter to pay the half-shekel tax with a coin found in a fish's
mouth. The tax under discussion was paid, prior to 70 CE, to the
Jerusalem temple. But after Jerusalem's defeat in 70, when
Matthew's Gospel was written, the emperor Vespasian co-opted it
as a punitive tax on Jews. He used it, insultingly, to rebuild and
maintain the temple of Jupiter Capitolinus in Rome, thereby
reminding Jews not only of Rome's superior power, but also of
Jupiter's superiority to the God of Israel. Paying the tax was
humiliating.

Jesus' conversation with Peter about paying the tax reframes its
significance. Jesus reminds Peter in verses 25 and 26 of the well-

known taxing ways of kings and emperors. Everyone pays taxes except the rulers' children. Not paying the tax is not an option because it will bring reprisals (17:27*a*). Instead, Jesus instructs Peter to catch a fish and find there the coin to pay the tax.

The key to understanding Jesus' instruction is found in the Gospel's previous scenes involving fish. Twice in chapters 14 and 15 Jesus has exerted God's sovereignty over fish, multiplying several small fish to feed large crowds. Contrary to Rome's claims that the emperor rules the sea, owns all its creatures, and tightly controls and taxes the fishing industry, the Gospel asserts that the sea and its creatures belong to God and are subject to God's sovereignty (recall Gen. 1:9-13, 20-23). God supplies the fish with the coin in its mouth. The coin expresses God's sovereignty. Disciples pay the tax. It appears to Rome that they are submissive and compliant. But for disciples the tax coin has a special significance. It testifies to God's sovereignty. The tax that is supposed to enact and acknowledge Rome's control has been reframed. Unbeknown to Rome, but known to Jesus' followers, it bears witness to God's reign. Paying the tax is an ambiguous act, an expression of hidden protest.

3. Flattery and Submission to Rome

In Romans 13:1-7, Paul instructs the churches in the empire's capital city to be "subject to the governing authorities" (13:1). He provides a theological reason. Three times in verses 1 and 2 he seems to flatter Rome by declaring that its governing authority is "from God," "instituted" and "appointed" by God. Three times in the next four verses he calls them "God's servants," who reward good conduct, punish bad conduct, and rule "for your good" (13:3-5). In verses 6 and 7 he gives some examples of "subject" behavior.

That this is flattery is evident from some cracks in Paul's extremely positive presentation. It seems strange that while presenting beneficent, divinely authorized rulers who supposedly always seek the good, he recognizes in verse 2 that some rebel against the authorities. But he does not explore why they rebel if the authorities are so just. And in verse 7, the section ends with Paul exhorting, "Fear for whom fear is due" (author's trans.). Why does he exhort "fear" when he has said that those who subject themselves do not fear because rulers reward good behavior (13:3)?

The cracks suggest that Paul knows that this is not the whole story. He does not engage the complexity of the issue and leaves important questions unaddressed. He does not consider, for example, governing authorities who do not carry out God's will, who oppose God's purposes, and who do not do justice "for your good."

Further, this flattering exhortation to submission in 13:1-7 does not cohere well with what Paul has said previously in Romans. In 1:18-32 he described the hostile and corrupt Gentile world subject to God's wrath. But here the governing authorities seem untouched by "the present evil age" and are designated agents of, not subjects of, God's wrath. In 8:18-25, Paul's eschatological perspective emphasizes that God will end this present evil age and establish God's purposes; 13:11-12 repeat this emphasis. But it is not mentioned in 13:1-7. In 12:2 he told them not to "be conformed to this world," but now he urges subjection to its ruling authorities. In 12:2*b* he told the believers to "discern what is the will of God," but he does not include discernment in 13:1-7. In 12:14-21 he recognized inevitable conflict with neighbors and that hostility can meet doing good (living out God's purposes), yet in 13:3 he (naively?) claims that rulers recognize and reward good behavior. In 12:17-21 he declares that God punishes evil, yet in 13:4 he identifies the governing authorities as agents of God's punishment.

Paul's own experiences indicate that flattery is not his only way of negotiating Rome's official representatives and it is frequently inappropriate. He has experienced imprisonments and beatings (2 Cor. 11:23, 25), the latter referring to a punishment inflicted by Roman officials (in contrast to synagogue officials in verse 24). Acts presents Paul as being beaten and imprisoned in Philippi (Acts 16:23-40), and nearly tortured by whipping in Acts 22:24-29. He recognizes that the ruling authorities oppose God's purposes and are under God's judgment (1 Cor. 2:6-8; 1 Thess. 5:3). He knows that believers cannot give their ultimate loyalty or nondiscerning submission to the empire because for believers there is one Lord. Paul reminded the Roman believers of their commitment in Romans 10:9 (cf. 1 Cor 8:5-6; 12:3).

Paul's theological thinking, shaped by eschatological and christological perspectives, sets Roman power in the context of God's greater triumphant purposes. Paul's eschatological convictions concern his confidence that God will end this present world and age, and establish God's just and life-giving purposes in full (see chapter 6, above). Believers are defined not by belonging to Rome's empire, but to God's purposes. Their ultimate political loyalty and homeland is with God. In discussing Philippians we saw that he sharply distinguishes the believers' identity from Roman claims about citizenship and the emperor as savior (see chapter 4, above). "*Our* citizenship is in heaven, and it is from there that *we* are expecting a Savior" (emphasis added; Phil. 3:20).

Paul's christological convictions center on Christ crucified (1 Cor. 2:2). Rome used crucifixion as the torture and death penalty for low-status rebels (against Rome's control); robbers (who attacked elite property); rebellious slaves (essential elite labor and property); and others that threatened the Roman order. Rome crucified provincials but not citizens, except for treason. Crucifixion thus defended elite structures and values. It was performed publicly to deter, intimidate, and coerce. Jesus had been crucified as a kingly pretender whose message and actions threatened the Roman status quo. To proclaim "Christ crucified" as Paul did was to announce a politically threatening message. But it also announced the limits of Roman power since Paul proclaimed Jesus as raised from the dead (Rom. 10:9; 1 Cor. 15). Rome's power could not prevent the imminent establishment of God's purposes.

These factors suggest that in Romans 13:1-7 Paul is choosing to present Rome in a flattering way because of some particular circumstances the church was experiencing. Scholars have made numerous guesses about the situation that might warrant such a flattering presentation.

- Perhaps some believers saw themselves as agents of God's judgment against the empire. Paul warns against violent action. Some have suggested that about ten years later the fire of 64 CE may have resulted from Christians who saw themselves hastening the day of judgment. If this is correct (and we do not know that it is), they would exhibit the sort of action Paul rejects here. Clearly they would have ignored Paul's instruction.
- Perhaps in the midst of widespread disgruntlement in the 50s

with the emperor Nero's harsh taxes (Tacitus, *Ann.* 13.50-51), Paul warns believers against not paying taxes. A refusal might provoke reprisals against Rome's Jewish community, including Jewish believers, already vulnerable to anti-Jewish sentiments.

- Perhaps, since Paul plans to visit Rome (1:11-15; 15:22-29), he thinks it necessary to defend himself against perceptions that his gospel about the establishment of God's purposes encourages disloyal actions against Rome.
- Perhaps Paul fears that Jewish Christians might inappropriately support growing tensions between Judeans and Rome, causing problems for the Christian communities in Rome.

All of these possibilities are guesses because Paul does not identify the situation he addresses. The guesses recognize, though, that these verses relate to a specific situation for which his flattering rhetoric is appropriate. Paul's instructions in Romans 13:1-7 are not a full description of his understanding of Rome's empire as we have seen. Although he exhorts subjection, he elsewhere recognizes the greater claim of God's purposes for believers, God's inevitable and imminent triumph, a world and rulers under judgment, the alternative practices of communities of believers, and the inevitable difficulties believers will experience in being faithful to God's purposes. These verses do not comprise a political treatise that presents a fixed ethic of submission for every situation.

Conclusion

In this chapter we have explored some of the dynamics involved in resisting Rome's rule. Often accommodation and resistance coexist. Resistance takes different forms. It can be violent and nonviolent, hidden and open, directly confrontational or more concerned with the distinctive practices and theology of an alternative community. It can imagine Rome's violent overthrow, employ disguised and ambiguous protest, and use flattery. Throughout this book we have observed some of the complex and diverse ways that the New Testament writings negotiate the Roman imperial world.

Postscript

It is virtually impossible to engage a topic such as the one discussed in this book without thinking about events in our own world. The term *empire* has been widely used to describe the role and actions of the United States in extending its power throughout the world by various means. It has also been used to describe multinational corporations that extend their enormous reach across the globe. In some respects our experience of empire is very different from the first century. We have different political systems. We can participate in elections, write letters to elected officials, and campaign for a particular candidate. We know a different history that has struggled for basic human rights. Yet our world is strangely similar. We know the importance of military power to securing influence. We know a world in which a relatively small percentage of the very rich control and consume much more than their share of the wealth. We know that government lies often in the hands of the elite who make decisions often to secure their own interests. We know a world in which "spin" is very much the name of the game.

How might Christians—whether they live at the center of the world's most powerful empire ever, or who know the impact, reach, and power of such empires—engage these realities? Does our discussion of New Testament texts offer any help?

To engage such an important issue that confronts contemporary communities of faith and citizens of the global village requires much thought, conversation, and engagement with books that specifically focus on this contemporary question. That task is far beyond the span of this book. Here I will make six brief comments as a small contribution toward much more extensive conversation and inquiry. I readily recognize that the issues are much more complex and need much more attention than my all-too-brief remarks here.

1. The New Testament Is a Very Political Document

Our discussion of numerous New Testament texts shows how deeply intertwined are matters of religion and politics. We cannot dismiss the questions of how we live in a world of empire. We cannot ignore these questions by claiming that following Jesus concerns religion, not politics. The former embraces the latter. Two quick observations indicate that discipleship is a matter of politics.

First, Jesus was crucified by Rome's empire. This story is foundational for the Christian movement. His death has been of enormous importance for Christian people and has been understood in numerous ways. But no interpretation of its significance can change the fact that crucifixion was a political act and a very public act. It was a means of social control exercised by Rome to remove those who challenged its system and to intimidate the rest into submission.

And second, we have seen throughout the previous eight chapters that the New Testament writers were very interested in thinking through what being a follower of Jesus, crucified by Rome but raised by God, might mean in a world of empire. This is not a peripheral concern. It is fundamental to their understandings of how God's purposes might be lived out in God's world. As people who read and live these texts some two millennia later, it is our task to work out the implications of this concern for our world.

2. Negotiating Empires Is Complicated

This discussion of New Testament texts as negotiations of the Roman Empire shows that the task of negotiating imperial power is complicated. The New Testament texts do not offer one simple strategy. They offer diverse perspectives on Rome's empire, and various strategies for engaging it. The strategies stretch from demonizing it, anticipating God's judgment on it, and opposing it with defiant (but self-protective) nonviolent actions, to praying for it, submitting to it, and imitating it.

If we like things clear and simple, this diversity of strategies is very frustrating. If we want a single formula to fit all situations, we won't find it in the New Testament. This complexity, though, gives us pause. These writings from early Christians show how difficult it is to live in/with/under/against empires. My choice of four prepositions in this last sentence alone hints at the diverse negotiation that is needed to be faithful. The difficulty with empire arises in part because empires often make totalizing claims. They claim to exert complete sovereignty. They claim unrivaled power. They claim to know best. They have the means to accomplish their will regardless of what anyone else thinks. They demand allegiance. They sanction their actions with religious talk ("God bless America"). They cannot tolerate dissent.

For Christians these claims raise profound questions. Jesus' teaching points his followers to love for God as their supreme allegiance. That love is to be expressed in love for neighbor. And Christians know that Jesus himself challenged and collided with empire and was crucified by an empire. That is, empires raise questions of allegiance (To whom does the world belong?); identity (Who are we?); community (What sort of world do we want to inhabit? Who is our neighbor and how do we treat them?); and power (Who exercises it and to what end? Who benefits? Who pays?). These are big and difficult questions for which there are no simple answers. But they are questions that lead us into the heart of living out Christian claims. The New Testament writings set them on our agenda and invite us to wrestle with them also.

3. Unquestioning Submission Is Not the Bible's Only Way

As we have seen, parts of the New Testament writings instruct followers of Jesus to pray for the emperor and to submit to governing authorities. Christians have often appealed to this instruction as though it were the only stance followers of Jesus are to exhibit toward the government. Come what may, so the argument goes, Christians must obey. This view encourages a willing submission, a quick trust, and an unquestioning acceptance of government policies and decisions. Often Romans 13 is understood to mean that God has ordained whatever the government does and so it is to be accepted, not resisted. One consequence of this is that maintaining the social order or cooperation with it is seen to be the most important thing.

There is no denying that Romans 13 and 1 Peter 2 are part of the Christian scriptures. Whether Romans 13 offers such an all-embracing and compliant approach to political matters is debatable, as I suggested in the last chapter. But one thing is not debatable. The New Testament writings do not offer only one strategy of compliance and submission to define how Christians might engage political matters. They do not endorse the current societal structure as unassailable. They do not make it sacred and untouchable as God-ordained. They do not endorse the status quo regardless of its wrongs. Some Christians have wrongly tried to assert such claims in the face of sinful realities such as slavery, or misogyny, or racism. The discussion in the previous chapters show that these early Christian writers willingly evaluated the Roman Empire and were not reluctant to declare it generally inconsistent with God's purposes. They do not urge blind submission to it. Instead, the discussion in the previous chapters shows that they frequently urged strategies of opposition and challenge, of contesting and subversion. Our New Testament writings challenge a "default position" of unswerving submission.

The issue, of course, is to know when to employ which strategy. When is compliance and when is resistance appropriate? That process of discernment is difficult. It involves, I would suggest, much prayer, study, thought, and debate.

4. Constant Opposition Is Not the Bible's Only Way

This is the opposite side of the coin. Just as we cannot always assume a submissive relationship, nor can we always assume an oppositional stance. The New Testament writings show a deep embeddedness in the world of empire and a profound realization of their limited ability to influence it. Jesus uses metaphors of empire to describe God's ways of working. He talks of the "empire or kingdom of God." He announces the coming triumph of God in which God's ways violently and forcibly overcome Rome. Paul writes in a similar vein. He readily employs military metaphors to describe Christian existence. Sometimes empires, including God's empire, accomplish good things. Empires can be ambiguous and we cannot pretend that we are not often beneficiaries of the ways of empire.

Again the issue is to know which strategy to employ. When is opposition and when is support appropriate? That process of discernment questions our default positions.

5. Active Nonviolence, Not Violence

The New Testament texts are consistent in rejecting human violence as a way of negotiating empires. Violence is reserved for God and for God's future intervention. It is forbidden to humans to employ violence in the present. But the absence of violence does not mean the absence of dissent and opposition. The third way comprises active, nonviolent, calculated interventions that reverse the destructive impact of empire.

These emphases raise huge questions about the use of military violence in our contemporary world as an instrument of empire. They raise enormous questions about the church's involvement in and frequent support for military action. My hunch is that this is an area that will take much courage for us to engage.

6. Alternative Worldviews and Communities

Perhaps this element forms the most frequent recurring theme throughout this study of the New Testament texts. The New Testament writers offer followers of Jesus an alternative understanding of the world as belonging not to an empire or political party or system, but as belonging to God. They offer followers of Jesus an understanding of themselves as claimed by God's love and as agents of God's life-giving purposes. They challenge and invite and shape Christian communities to become places that embody God's purposes and that embody an alternative way of being human in the midst of the empire.

These strategies of reconceptualization and of alternative social experiences and relationships result, in part, from the early Christians not having any access to power and no opportunity to make systemic changes. This, of course, is one major difference between our world and theirs. Just exactly what Jesus or Paul or Matthew or Mark or Luke or James would say to us is not immediately obvious. At least, our different situation raises important questions about how we use access to power, and what vision of society we promote through it. Do we promote purposes of exclusion and hate or of the inclusion of all people in God's life-giving purposes? It also brings the challenge that communities of faith carefully and faithfully discern God's purposes and embody them in their own living.

What is involved in such discernment? Perhaps the topics of our eight chapters provide some guidelines for areas in which we need to do some thinking and discussing in order to develop appropriate strategies for faithful engagement.

1. The discussion of chapter 1 suggests that it would be important for us to understand the nature and structures of our contemporary empires.

2. The discussion of chapter 2 indicates our responsibility to evaluate our contemporary empires theologically in terms of God's declared purpose to bless all the families or nations of the earth (Gen. 12:1-3). How do they measure up to those purposes?

3. The discussion of chapter 3 urges us to discern the current faces of empire to identify aspects of life in which we need to negotiate the demands and claims of empire. One of the reasons for such discernment is to prevent us from taking for granted what we experience each day as though "it is just the way things are."

4. The discussion of chapter 4 turns our attention to the impact of empire on rural and urban life. How does it affect these areas?

5. The discussion of chapter 5 invites us to examine the roles of "religious" places, groups, and leaders in empires. What alliances exist with the empire, and are those alliances life giving or death bringing?

6. The discussion of chapter 6 presses this inquiry further to include the role of religious sanctions or theological rationales. In what ways are churches allies, agents, or willing partners with empire? How compromised are we? What theological claims are used to justify or to oppose empire?

7. The discussion of chapter 7 focuses on the ways in which economics, food supplies, and disease relate to imperial power. What is the relation between our capitalist quest for more and greater profit and imperial structures? Despite God's will for hungry people to be fed, hunger remains a significant problem in this country and the world. Access to medical care varies greatly throughout the world.

8. The discussion of chapter 8 invites us to think about appropriate ways of intervening to oppose and redress the destructive ways and impacts of empire when they do not measure up to God's purposes.

Every one of these areas needs much more consideration and no doubt there are numerous other dimensions to be engaged as well. But they provide something of a framework for consideration and an agenda for ecclesial communities to pursue in forming alternative worldviews and communities that embody alternative, anti-imperial practices.

Bibliography

Arlandson, James M. *Women, Class, and Society in Early Christianity: Models from Luke-Acts.* Peabody, MA: Hendrickson, 1997.

Bauckham, Richard. "The Economic Critique of Rome in Revelation 18." In *The Climax of Prophecy: Studies on the Book of Revelation.* Edinburgh: T & T Clark, 1993.

Blasi, Anthony J. et al., eds. *Handbook of Early Christianity: Social Science Approaches.* Walnut Creek, CA: AltaMira Press, 2002.

Carter, Warren. "Are There Imperial Texts in the Class? Intertextual Eagles and Matthean Eschatology as 'Lights Out' Time for Imperial Rome (Matthew 24:27-31)." *Journal of Biblical Literature* 122 (2003): 467-87.

———. "Constructions of Violence and Identities in Matthew's Gospel." In *Violence in the New Testament,* edited by Shelly Matthews and Leigh Gibson, 81-108. London: T & T Clark, 2005.

———. "Honoring the Emperor and Sacrificing Wives and Slaves: 1 Peter 2:13–3:6." In *A Feminist Companion to the General Epistles,* edited by A.-J. Levine, 13-43. London: T & T Clark, 2004.

———. *Households and Discipleship: A Study of Matthew 19–20.* JSNT Sup. 103. Sheffield, UK: Sheffield Academic Press, 1994.

———. "Imperial Paradigms in the Parables of Matthew 18:21-35 and 22:1-14." *Interpretation* 56 (2002): 260-72.

———. *Matthew and Empire: Initial Explorations.* Harrisburg, PA: Trinity Press International, 2001.

144

————. "Matthew and the Gentiles: Individual Conversion and/or Systemic Transformation." *JSNT* 26 (2004): 259-82.

————. *Matthew and the Margins: A Sociopolitical and Religious Reading.* Maryknoll, NY: Orbis, 2000.

————. *Pontius Pilate: Portraits of a Roman Governor.* Collegeville, MN: Liturgical Press, 2003.

————. "Proclaiming (in/against) Empire Then and Now," *Word and World* 25 (2005): 149-58.

Crossan, John Dominic, and Jonathan L. Reed. *In Search of Paul: How Jesus's Apostle Opposed Rome's Empire with God's Kingdom.* San Francisco: HarperSanFrancisco, 2004.

De Vos, Craig Steven. *Church and Community Conflicts: The Relationships of the Thessalonian, Corinthian, and Philippian Churches with Their Wider Civic Communities.* SBLDS 168. Atlanta: Scholars Press, 1999.

Garnsey, Peter. *Cities, Peasants, and Food in Classical Antiquity.* Pages 226-52. Cambridge: Cambridge University Press, 1988.

————. *Food and Society in Classical Antiquity.* Pages 1-61. Cambridge: Cambridge University Press, 1999.

Garnsey, Peter, and Richard Saller. *The Roman Empire: Economy, Society, and Culture.* Berkeley: University of California Press, 1987.

Gill, David, and Conrad Gempf, eds. *The Book of Acts in Its Graeco-Roman Setting.* Grand Rapids: Eerdmans, 1993.

Hanson, K. C., and Douglas E. Oakman. *Palestine in the Time of Jesus.* Minneapolis: Fortress Press, 1998.

Herzog II, William R. *Jesus, Justice, and the Reign of God.* Louisville: Westminster John Knox Press, 2000.

————. *Parables as Subversive Speech: Jesus as Pedagogue of the Oppressed.* Louisville: Westminster John Knox Press, 1994.

Horsley, Richard A. *Jesus and Empire: The Kingdom of God and the New World Disorder.* Minneapolis: Fortress Press, 2003.

————, ed. *Paul and Empire: Religion and Power in Roman Imperial Society.* Harrisburg, PA: Trinity Press International, 1997.

————, ed. *Paul and Politics: Ekklesia, Israel, Imperium, Interpretation.* Harrisburg, PA: Trinity Press International, 2000.

————, ed. *Paul and the Roman Imperial Order.* Harrisburg, PA: Trinity Press International, 2004.

Horsley, Richard A., and John S. Hanson. *Bandits, Prophets & Messiahs: Popular Movements in the Time of Jesus.* Harrisburg, PA: Trinity International, 1999.

Howard-Brook, Wes, and Anthony Gwyther. *Unveiling Empire: Reading Revelation Then and Now.* Maryknoll, NY: Orbis, 2001.

145

Huskinson, Janet, ed. *Experiencing Rome: Culture, Identity and Power in the Roman Empire.* London: Routledge Press, 2000.

Kautsky, John H. *The Politics of Aristocratic Empires.* Chapel Hill: University of North Carolina Press, 1982.

Lenski, Gerhard E. *Power and Privilege: A Theory of Social Stratification.* Chapel Hill: University of North Carolina Press, 1984.

Myers, Ched. *Binding the Strong Man: A Political Reading of Mark's Story of Jesus.* Maryknoll, NY: Orbis, 1988.

Neyrey, Jerome H., ed. *The Social World of Luke-Acts.* Peabody, MA: Hendrickson, 1991.

Oakes, Peter, ed. *Rome in the Bible and the Early Church.* Grand Rapids: Baker, 2002.

Pilgrim, Walter E. *Uneasy Neighbors: Church and State in the New Testament.* Minneapolis: Fortress Press, 1999.

Price, S. R. F. *Rituals and Power: The Roman Imperial Cult in Asia Minor.* Cambridge: Cambridge University Press, 1984.

Rohrbaugh, Richard L., ed. *The Social Sciences and New Testament Interpretation.* Peabody, MA: Hendrickson, 1996.

Saldarini, Anthony J. *Pharisees, Scribes, and Sadducees in Palestinian Society.* Grand Rapids: Eerdmans, 2001.

Scott, James. *Domination and the Arts of Resistance.* New Haven: Yale University Press, 1990.

————. *Weapons of the Weak: Everyday Forms of Peasant Resistance.* New Haven: Yale University Press, 1985.

Stambaugh, John E., and David L. Balch, *The New Testament in Its Social Environment.* Philadelphia: Westminster Press, 1986.

Stegemann, Wolfgang et al., eds. *The Social Setting of Jesus and the Gospels.* Minneapolis: Fortress Press, 2002.

Tamez, Elsa. *The Scandalous Message of James: Faith Without Works Is Dead.* New York: Crossroads, 1992.

Van Tilborg, Sjef. *Reading John in Ephesus.* Leiden: E. J. Brill, 1996.

Wengst, Klaus. *Pax Romana and the Peace of Jesus Christ.* Philadelphia: Fortress Press, 1987.

Whittaker, C. R. "The Poor." In *The Romans,* edited by Andrea Giardina, 272-99. Chicago: University of Chicago Press, 1993.

Williams, David J. *Paul's Metaphors: Their Context and Character.* Peabody, MA: Hendrickson, 1999.

Zanker, Paul. *The Power of Images in the Age of Augustus.* Ann Arbor: University of Michigan Press, 1988.

Bibliography of Classical Works Cited

Augustus. "Res Gestae," or "Acts of Augustus." In W. Eck, *Augustus*.
    Oxford: Blackwell Publishing, 2003. Translated by Deborah
    Lucas Schneider; "Res Gestae/Acts of Augustus." Translated by
    S. A. Takács.
Cicero. "De provinciis consularibus." In *Cicero*. 28 volumes. Vol. 13.
    Translated by Robert Gardner. Loeb Classical Library.
    Cambridge, MA: Harvard University Press, 1958.
Josephus. "Vita," "The Jewish War," and "Jewish Antiquities." In
    Josephus. 13 volumes. Translated by H. St. J. Thackeray, Ralph
    Marcus, and Louis H. Feld. Loeb Classical Library. Cambridge,
    MA: Harvard University Press, 1926–63.
Origen. *Homilies on Genesis and Exodus*. Translated by Ronald E. Heine.
    Washington, DC: Catholic University Press, 1982.
Philo. "De Specibus Legibus." In *Philo*. 11 volumes. Vol. 7. Translated by
    F. H. Colsen. Loeb Classical Library. Cambridge, MA: Harvard
    University Press, 1937.
———. "The Embassy to Gaius." In *Philo*. 11 volumes. Vol. 10. Translated
    by F. H. Colsen. Loeb Classical Library. Cambridge, MA:
    Harvard University Press, 1962.
Suetonius. "The Deified Vespasian." In *Suetonius*. 2 volumes. Vol. 2.
    Translated by J. C. Rolfe. Loeb Classical Library. Cambridge,
    MA: Harvard University Press, 1913–14.
Tacitus. "Histories." In *Tacitus*. 5 volumes. Vol. 2. Translated by Clifford
    H. Moore. Loeb Classical Library. Cambridge, MA: Harvard
    University Press, 1925.

Tertullian. "De Idololatria." In J. H. Waszink and J. C. M. van Winden, *De Idololatria*. Leiden and New York: E. J. Brill, 1987.

Virgil. "Aeneid." In *Virgil*. 2 volumes. Vol. 1. Translated by H. Rushton Fairclough; revised by G. P. Goold. Loeb Classical Library. Cambridge, MA: Harvard University Press, 1916–18; revised 1999.